PRAYING WITH OUR FEET

ENCOUNTERING GOD IN THE MARGINS

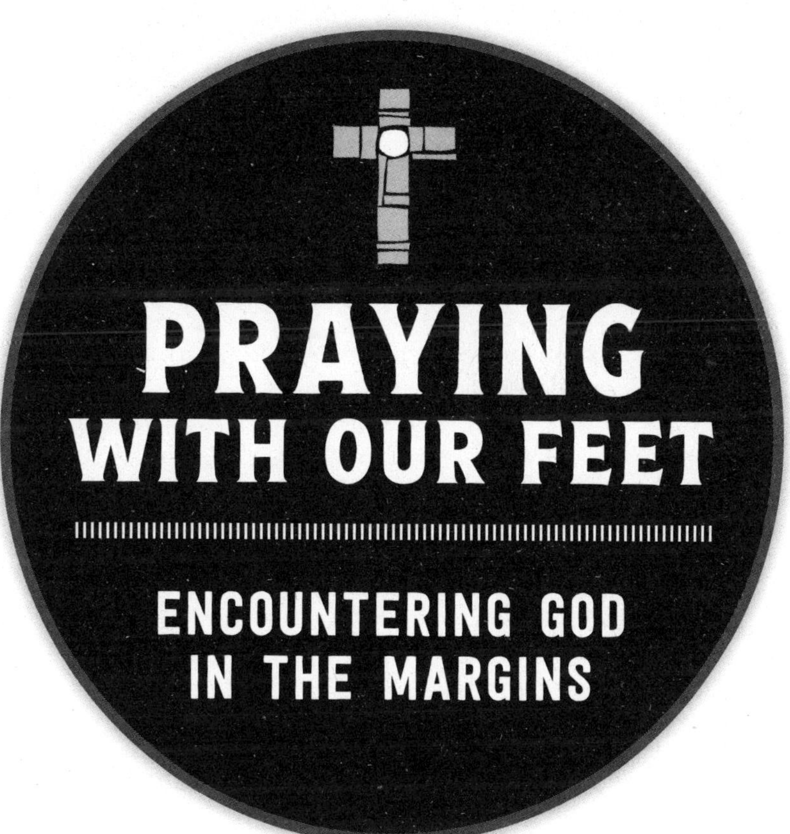

PRAYING WITH OUR FEET

ENCOUNTERING GOD IN THE MARGINS

ANSEL AUGUSTINE, DMin

LOYOLAPRESS.
A JESUIT MINISTRY

LOYOLA PRESS.
A JESUIT MINISTRY
www.loyolapress.com

Cover art credit: Mai Vu/iStock/Getty Images, CSA Images/Vetta/Getty

ISBN: 978-0-8294-5879-4
Library of Congress Control Number: 2025932644

Published in Chicago, IL
Printed in the United States of America
25 26 27 28 29 30 31 32 33 34 Versa 10 9 8 7 6 5 4 3 2 1

*"**Peace is the fruit of justice. . . .** We must work with all who strive to make available the fruits of creation to all God's children everywhere. It was in chains that our parents were brought to these shores and in violence we were maintained in bondage. Let us who are the children of pain now be a bridge of reconciliation. Let us who are the offspring of violence become the channels of compassion. Let us, the sons and daughters of bondage, be the bringers of peace."*

—"What We Have Seen and Heard:
A Pastoral Letter on Evangelization from
the Black Bishops of the United States"

CONTENTS

FOREWORD

A MAN OF DEEP FAITH

Dr. Augustine is a man of deep faith. He loves the Church and sees the potential for influencing society away from its ills by means of her renowned social teaching, from which he has discovered his own passion for a better Church and a better world, where the love-of-neighbor ethic of the gospel of Jesus Christ can hold sway.

Praying with Our Feet is a book that follows upon a wealth of personal experience and ministry served in the trenches of urban life. Dr. Augustine's first loves are youth ministry and young adult ministry, from where he knows the hearts and dreams of young people, their questions, and their critiques of the current adult generation. He knows the tough terrain that is the Church and her inner workings, her saints and sinners. He has a firsthand knowledge of the even tougher terrain that is American society and its institutions—a society seemingly comfortable with demarcations that maintain rigid boundaries between the haves and the have-nots, the rich and the poor.

It is interesting to note how relatively recent are the notions of human dignity and social justice for all as concepts for social ordering and praxis. The twentieth century has bred much of this in wake of the horrors foisted upon us by war, mass destruction, and calculated human extermination. But then the human condition still reeks of sin. Despite some real gains in social progress here and there, far too often, and just when we thought society was shedding some of its past sins, some awful incident erupts, wreaking havoc and agony, forcing us to wonder how much things really have changed for the better.

President Abraham Lincoln stunned the nation with his iconic 1863 Gettysburg Address pronouncing that America was conceived with the belief in the proposition that *All men are created equal.* It may have been the first time many Americans ever heard of the premise. As Americans, we want to believe that all people are created equal even if we are less likely to treat them that way. Suffice it to say, "equality" is a meddlesome term for our democratic experiment. Many opinions abound that would attempt to define it or undo it. Other nations would call us on the carpet as to how truly and faithfully we have lived up to this piece of civil doctrine. It all has to do with what is called the *mysterium iniquitatis*—the mystery of evil—that burglarizes the best inclinations of the human spirit.

In this vein, Dr. Augustine carefully explicates a path for systemic change. Out of the ground of his love for the Church he has earned a right to press the question why we are indifferent to becoming a more just and equitable society. He introduces us to some of his mentors over the years, church leaders who have left behind legacies of service, evangelization, and advocacy for the poor and for people pushed to the sides. He delves into the mess of the human situation appealing to the best that is found in the human spirit—those parts of us that can right the wrongs of injustice, ensconced preferential bias, racism, poverty, and societal neglect. He shows us how we can tailor our democratic structures so that people striving to live wholesome, holistic lives can thrive.

We are a proud nation. We believe we have the answers to the world's problems, but we fail to probe the inequities of our own social and governmental systems that keep us strangers to one another, provoking fear, crime, family instability, and despair. Our hyper sense of privacy is our undoing, preventing us from a workable solidarity and an appreciation of the noble forces that can prioritize the common good.

Praying with Our Feet makes for an informative read for people engaged in ministry. This book can be useful as an instructional text for people working in Catholic Charities and St. Vincent de Paul ministry. It poses rich meditation for parish small group discussion, for workers involved in social justice ministries, and for people wishing to know more about the Church's teachings on human dignity and equality and social justice. Dr. Augustine's book is a rich companion resource for classroom instruction on various social teachings and social justice topics.

—Bishop Joseph N. Perry
Auxiliary Bishop Emeritus of Chicago

Titular Bishop of Lead

Chairman of thc USCCB
Committee Against Racism

Former Chairman of the USCCB
Subcommittee on American Affairs

PREFACE

TWO MEN WHO PRAYED WITH THEIR FEET

A lesson from St. Ignatius about love being not a noun but a verb was imparted to me by one of my most treasured mentors in ministry, the late Bishop Fernand Cheri III, OFM. St. Ignatius famously said *Love is shown more in deeds than in words.*[1] But the full meaning of this philosophy was driven home to me when I witnessed the way that Bishop Cheri lived his life. He led by his example of love.

I met Bishop Cheri—then Fr. "Ferd"—in the summer of 2000 at the Institute for Black Catholic Studies at Xavier University of Louisiana, where I was working on my Certificate in Youth Ministry. I had recently earned an undergraduate degree from Loyola University New Orleans and was working at a radio station and record company with my heart set on my dream job of becoming a disc jockey. Then, something happened. After chaperoning a youth *lock-in* at my home parish, St. Peter Claver, I fell in love with ministry.

After seeking the wisdom of another mentor, my pastor, the late Fr. Michael Jacques, SSE, I changed my undergraduate major from mass communications to sociology. My plan was to pursue a master's of pastoral studies at Loyola's Institute for Ministry while also working toward a certificate in youth ministry at the Institute for Black Catholic Studies at Xavier University of Louisiana.

As I began my ministry studies at Xavier, two things shocked me: I was the youngest person in the program by about twenty years, and I was constantly being recruited by all the priests to enter the seminary! Initially this felt like an honor, but it soon became aggravating when it appeared that my dedication to full-time youth ministry was not valued or seen as relevant.

One morning after class, I went to the chapel. As I sat in the back, catching up on my homework in the peace and quiet before Mass, I met Fr. Ferd. He stood out not only because he was dressed in the Franciscan habit but also because his friendliness was without constraint. “How you doin’, bro?” he asked. He introduced himself and then asked about my background, or, as we say here in New Orleans, he was fishing to find out who “my people” are. After a few minutes of small talk, he asked, “Have you ever thought of becoming a priest?” In my mind, I was like, *Here we go again! Could a brother get a break and just be a great youth minister? Is priesthood the only option for single men who feel a call to ministry?* I responded, “Father, I don’t think my girlfriend will let me go to seminary unless she can come too.” He gave me his famous chuckle which I would grow to love (and now miss) so much.

As with many things, God works in unique ways. Over the years Fr. Ferd and I became good friends, connecting whenever possible and eventually collaborating on a few ministry projects during his brief stint as one of the campus ministers at Xavier University of Louisiana, and once again when he was serving as Auxiliary Bishop of the Archdiocese of New

Orleans. In my position as Director of the Office of Black Catholic Ministries, I reported to none other than Bishop Ferd; however, our relationship was deeper than the formality of an employee/supervisor dynamic. We were family. I jokingly referred to him as Uncle Ferd, just like his nephew, Richie Cheri, was accustomed to doing.

Bishop Ferd was a compassionate visionary. A Franciscan to the core, he reveled in hospitality and had love for everyone, especially the marginalized. And he never stopped advocating for Black Catholics. Although he exuded the hospitality that his religious order is known for, his spirituality also reflected the Spiritual Exercises of St. Ignatius, with its emphasis on the value of God's love and our call to respond to God's love through love of neighbor. This perspective fueled his passion to work toward building a just society, one that guarantees inclusion and liberation for all.

Bishop Ferd's mentorship guided me through some of the darkest moments in my ministry. Too often, I struggled with a sense of hopelessness in my quest to meet the unique needs of Black Catholics through various national Catholic organizations. There were many gatherings at which I was the only person who either looked like me or thought like me. This reality had me causing, as the late John Lewis used to say, "good trouble." I was calling out gaps in programming and resources, or I was pointing out how decisions could either offend or ignore not only Black Catholics but also other groups of people existing on the peripheries. This good trouble would sometimes lead to isolation or intentional undermining by non-Blacks or by Black folks who were comfortable with the status quo. Naturally, it was during our emotional talks that Bishop Ferd and I would share our burdens of fighting the good fight, and then strategize and pray on what we should do in the next steps of our ministries. We really saw one another as partners in our unique ministries.

Bishop Cheri's presence helped me to affirm my purpose in life as an advocate for our Black youth and young adults. This has not been an easy road to traverse. I never expected that I would struggle to make progress with people in my own community. I was also surprised to find people in the larger Church community who are stuck in their ways—people who do not see, understand, or prioritize the unique needs of people of color. As a result of fighting for those on the peripheries, I have been labeled a troublemaker and have even been blackballed in my efforts to advocate for others. Along the way, I often witnessed Bishop Cheri, in his own pastoral manner, endure similar challenges. But he was a stellar example of persistence and fortitude in passionately forging ahead, all the time believing that God called him to be a bishop so that he could do what he was doing. It is this profound and inspiring witness from Bishop Ferd, and from other mentors, ancestors, and elders, that has enabled me to remain steadfast in the mission of God's call.

In 2020, Bishop Cheri was named the administrator of St. Peter Claver. He asked if I would return from a position I had taken in the Archdiocese of Washington to help him run the parish. Little did I know just how profoundly I would be living out St. Ignatius's ideology of expressing love in deeds more than in words. Within two months of my return to New Orleans, Hurricane Ida hit. Most people fled to safety, but Bishop Cheri insisted on staying and I remained with him. I was glad I stayed because the next day, after the power had gone out, Bishop Cheri decided it would be wise for us to leave the city and we ended up in Montgomery, Alabama, along with Fr. Manuel Williams and the Resurrection Catholic Church family. Always the visionary, Bishop Cheri was full of creative ideas for how to rebuild the community and renew the Church after the storm. We worked together over the next month traveling between Montgomery and New Orleans to rebuild the neighborhood and community following the storm. This was done through collecting gift cards and donations from around the country to help local families buy the supplies they needed to repair their homes, along with other necessary supplies. Bishop Cheri's voice and reputation assisted with garnering larger support. We not only helped the St. Peter Claver community, but other neighborhoods as well with these efforts. Bishop Cheri's vision during the crisis affirmed my mindset to never fear dreaming out loud.

Bishop Cheri embodied the spirit of a phrase coined by Rabbi Abraham Joshua Heschel, who participated in the Selma, Alabama, civil rights movement: *Praying with our feet.*

Unfortunately, within a year, Bishop Cheri fell ill. For the next several months, he was in and out of the hospital. People closest to him were urging him to rest, but he used this time to stubbornly and faithfully fulfill his ministerial duties. Eventually he was admitted to the hospital and placed under hospice care until he passed. During those last weeks of his life, and even though he was unable to communicate, I spent as much time with him as I could, experiencing many moments of prayer and sacredness in his company. It was a small way for me to show love to a man who had shown great love to me, and to so many others, all throughout his life.

Bishop Cheri embodied the spirit of a phrase coined by Rabbi Abraham Joshua Heschel, who participated in the Selma, Alabama, civil rights movement: *Praying with our feet.* I learned about praying with our feet from my other mentor and former pastor, Fr. Michael Jacques, SSE. Before coming to New Orleans, Fr. Mike had worked in Selma at the Edmundite Southern Mission, where he picked up Rabbi Heschel's memorable way of describing how we put our faith into action. From this perspective, Rabbi Heschel was in agreement with St. Ignatius with his clear grasp that love is, in fact, shown more in deeds than in words. And so too was Bishop Cheri in alignment with the Ignatian way. This was the life that Bishop Cheri embodied.

As Catholics, the notion of praying with our feet is captured in what is known as the "Two Feet of Love in Action."[2] The first "foot" is charity, which centers on alleviating immediate suffering. The second "foot" is social action, which involves transforming structures and systems that cause such suffering. Catholic social teaching identifies the principles of this social action accordingly:

- **Dignity of the Human Person:** we are called to ask whether our actions as a society respect or threaten the life and dignity of the human person.
- **Family, Community, and Participation:** we are called to support the family, which is the principle social institution, so that people can participate in society, build a community spirit, and promote the well-being of all.
- **Rights and Responsibilities:** we are called to protect the human rights of all people, such as the right to food, clothing, housing, and healthcare.

- **Option for the Poor and Vulnerable:** we are called to pay special attention to the needs of those who are poor and vulnerable, and we are encouraged to put their needs first.
- **The Dignity of Work and the Rights of Workers:** we are called to protect the basic rights of all workers, such as the right to engage in productive work, fair wages, private property, and the right to organize, join unions, and pursue economic opportunity.
- **Solidarity:** we are called to recognize that, because God is our Father, we are all brothers and sisters, with the responsibility to care for one another.
- **Care for God's Creation:** we are called to care for all that God has made.

Each of us is "missioned" to live out our baptismal call of creating a just society. Throughout his pontificate, Pope Francis has challenged us to keep the marginalized of society at the forefront. In this book, I am going to explore the intimate connections between the principles of Catholic social teaching and the Spiritual Exercises of St. Ignatius, which outlines the transformative process of deepening one's relationship with God.

As you read this book, my prayer is that you are affirmed and inspired to use your unique gifts to make the world, especially your community, better for everyone, but above all for those who are oppressed. We are all called to be a voice for those who have not been afforded the privilege of speaking for themselves, and to create safe spaces in which they can do so.

This is the life that Bishop Cheri led; he didn't just talk the talk, he walked the walk. In the tradition of St. Ignatius,

Bishop Cheri was a person who lived for others; his love for everyone is something he modeled every day of his life, even amid criticism and disrespect by those he was serving. I am grateful to have been mentored by a servant of God who really did give his life for the Church. Someone who prayed with his feet in service of those most in need.

May each of us pray with our feet and express our love through deeds more than words.

I am known for having a profound appreciation of and passion for handwoven tapestries, specifically the beadwork of my Black Masking Mardi Gras Indian culture of New Orleans, because tapestries and beadwork memorialize the unique histories of cultures lived out on the margins of society. Thus, when I talk about the fabric of our society, I'm not simply utilizing a familiar metaphor. What gets sewn into the fabric of our society really matters to me, and I think about it in literal terms. I am acutely aware that the decisions we are making have the potential to weave beauty, integrity, and dignity into the fabric of society, and we should capitalize on every opportunity to weave a lovely tapestry of life for ourselves and for future generations.

—Ansel Augustine, DMin

CHAPTER 1

GOD IS CALLING YOU

Spiritual awakenings typically involve two concurrent realizations: First, God's grace is amazing, and second, I am not worthy. This dynamic, of course, is captured in the beloved traditional Christian hymn, "Amazing Grace," written by a former enslaver, John Newton. Newton wrote the song after experiencing a radical awakening to the reality of the evilness of slavery, an insight that gave birth to his moral and spiritual transformation. This song proclaims how amazing God's grace is and immediately follows with the acknowledgment of unworthiness ("that saved a wretch like me"). In other words, spiritual awakenings bring us eyeball-to-eyeball with grace and sin. It is for this reason that, in the Christian tradition, the first stage of spiritual enlightenment is called *purgation*. When confronted with the awesomeness of God's grace, we become all too aware of our own sinfulness and seek to have it purged, just as fire purges the imperfections in metal.

In Hebrew, the word for *sin* technically means "missing the mark." Unfortunately, when we venture deeper into spiritual awakening, we miss the mark in our understanding of sin. We tend to focus too much on committing sins (which can evolve into a narcissistic scrupulosity) as opposed to our participation in sin. But there are two aspects to this concept of sin. In one, *sin* refers to our thoughts, words, and actions that are contrary to God's law of love. In the other, *sin* refers to the fallen condition of every human being. While our spiritual awakening compels us to deal with our own sins, it also urges us to deal with the realities of sin that surround us. In other words, God's love not only encourages us to be better people, it also encourages us to make the world a better place for all human beings.

The first week of St. Ignatius's Spiritual Exercises focuses on *purgation*, or the process of grappling with sin, both personal and global. This first week is all about conversion from sin, which is seen not as the breaking of a law but rather as the breach of our relationship with God and others. Purgation is not a one-and-done reality, nor is it a stage that we complete; rather, it is part of our ongoing personal conversion as well as part of our ongoing mission to call the world to conversion. The purifying fire of purgation always burns within the heart of a disciple.

Healing Sin through Service to Others

It wasn't until May of 2020, when I moved back to New Orleans to help Bishop Cheri with our home parish, that I realized the devastating impact of the COVID-19 pandemic on our city. Tourism, Louisiana's main source of income, was completely shut down. With very few jobs available, most people in the community were struggling to make ends meet.

Out of desperation, many resorted to stealing cars and, as a result, violence in New Orleans skyrocketed. Home was not as safe as it once was.

Community activists like me came together in response to the crisis. First up, we decided to have toy and food giveaways during the Christmas season. I was "voluntold" by the group to play Santa Claus and, despite high heat and humidity that had me sweating through my beard, wig, and suit, we were able to spread some joy throughout the various neighborhoods. Folks around the country donated toys, bikes, books, and clothing, and local grocery stores contributed food. It was a blessing to see joy in the eyes of the children, and hope in the eyes of their adults.

On Christmas day, following Mass at St. Peter Claver, I received a call from my friend and fellow community activist, Belden "Noonie Man" Batiste, who informed me about a young girl who did not receive anything for Christmas and was asking if Santa could bring her some toys. I said, "Of course!" Unfortunately, we did not have any toys left, so we went shopping the day after Christmas and loaded up. We were to meet the child and her family the next evening at the Treme Recreation Community Center in the Sixth Ward of New Orleans. I brought my goddaughter along so she could share in the Christmas cheer.

We pulled up to the Treme Center and I quickly threw on my Santa suit. I was unloading the gifts from my trunk when a car pulled up behind me. From within, I could hear a little girl screaming joyfully. As soon as the car stopped, she jumped out and ran over to give me a huge hug. "Santa," she said through her tears, "I thought you forgot about me!" I looked at my goddaughter and saw that she was also crying. After confirming from Santa that the multiple bags of presents were indeed for her, the little girl eagerly started opening the presents with the help of my goddaughter.

As she joyfully opened her presents, the little girl's uncle and aunt expressed their thanks to me and Noonie Man, and explained that the girl's dad and mom—a pimp and prostitute—were not in the girl's life as much as they would have liked to have been. Just then, another car pulled up and two young men got out. One of them, the passenger, was the girl's father. He told us how grateful he was for what we were doing. The driver, a young man with a full beard and head of hair, had been silently listening. "Mr. Ansel," he said, "Is that you?" I was surprised. Understand, I could barely see because the heat from the suit, wig, and beard had fogged up my glasses. "Yes, it's me," I said. He reminded me that he was one of my former students at St. Peter Claver Elementary School. He then told his friend, "Mr. Ansel can help you with your situation."

With this endorsement, the girl's father knew he could trust me. He let me know that he was homeless and destitute, having given up his way of life as a pimp in order to be in his daughter's life. He explained that the mother was not in the picture; she had abandoned their daughter immediately after childbirth. He then looked me directly in my eyes and said, "I'll turn myself in to the law if you promise to help take care of my daughter until I come home." Of course I was stunned by his proposal. Even so, it was not hard to decide what I should do. I knew that this was an opportunity to do what God wanted even if it caused a disturbance in my routine.

For the next few years, and even now as I write these words, several friends and I have been helping this girl, now a young lady, and her family. A few folks have asked why I would do such a thing. In response—and I take my inspiration from Pope Francis, who, when asked, "Who is Jorge Bergoglio?" responded, "I am a sinner whom God has looked upon"—I simply tell people this is the right thing to do whenever we are called to encounter any of God's children, especially those who may not be in our regular circle of friends and neighbors. While I am definitely not perfect—none of us are—we are never separated from God's love, grace, and mercy. Acknowledging without judging brokenness and sinfulness is not affirming the sin; it is the first step to healing. It is why we love others, and why service should be at the center of any ministry. We are called to see Christ in others.

We are called to see Christ in others.

The global COVID-19 pandemic served as a powerful reminder of our interconnectedness and the importance of unity in the face of shared challenges. As communities around the world grappled with the impacts of the virus, we witnessed countless acts of kindness, solidarity, and mutual support that transcended boundaries of race, religion, and nationality. Healthcare workers from diverse backgrounds joined forces to save lives, while neighbors from different walks of life rallied to support the most vulnerable among us. In these acts of unity, we caught a glimpse of the transformative power that can arise when we embrace our differences and work together toward a common goal.

Jesus Is Already There

When we go to the margins, we must remember that *we* are not bringing Jesus there; Jesus is *already* there. We must be ready to encounter him in the form he is taking in that place and time. We make progress in this work by recognizing that none of us are saviors. God, and only God, is our savior. In our Baptism we are called to bring his mercy and love to others. Remember, it is not about us. It is about what God does through us.

That day at the Treme Center when Santa brought Christmas gifts to a little girl, I could have judged the young man for his past choices, or I could have scolded my former student for being associated with someone who had led such a lifestyle, but I didn't. To quote Pope Francis—"Who am I to judge?"—I believe all of this was part of God's plan to heal this man by setting him on a path where he could rediscover his dignity and reconnect with his child. We are called to respond with love and compassion to all forms of evil in this world. When we do, it becomes possible to lead a community to conversion: the choice of a better path and the opportunities that become available when one commits to a life of discipleship in Christ.

In a world filled with people grappling with injustice and inequity, this question of *Who are we to judge* cuts to the heart of what it means to live a spiritual life. Too often, we compartmentalize our beliefs, confining them to the safe havens of our places of worship or the quiet corners of our minds. Yet, the profound teachings of Jesus Christ and the social justice principles woven throughout Catholic doctrine challenge us to embrace a faith whose words and rituals stir our hearts and compel us to confront the harsh realities that afflict the most vulnerable among us. In a world where billions live in abject poverty, where racism and discrimination fester like open wounds, where the cries of the oppressed echo (and are, at times, ignored) through the corridors of power, can we really claim to be following in the footsteps of Christ if we are averting our gaze? Can we call ourselves people of faith if our spiritual journey is untethered from the struggle for justice, equity, and human dignity?

Perhaps the greatest misconception we must contend with is the notion that spirituality and social justice are separate realms, distinct and unrelated. We are sometimes told that our faith is a personal matter, a private affair between ourselves and our Creator, and that delving into the messy complexities of societal ills is a distraction from our spiritual growth. This fallacy, perpetuated for centuries, has been used as justification for inaction and apathy in the face of systemic oppression.

> In a world where billions live in abject poverty, where racism and discrimination fester like open wounds, where the cries of the oppressed echo through the corridors of power, can we really claim to be following in the footsteps of Christ if we are averting our gaze?

The truth is that our spiritual lives and our commitment to justice are inextricably intertwined—they are two strands woven into the same tapestry. Rev. William J. Barber II, a prominent preacher and civil rights activist, once said, "Preachers don't get to opt out of politics; we can be chaplains of Empire or prophets of God."[3] I would not limit that sentiment to preachers but would expand it to include all disciples of Jesus Christ who, through Baptism, share in his prophetic ministry. The Gospels are replete with Christ's teachings on the inviolable dignity of every human being, his unwavering solidarity with the poor and marginalized, and his condemnation of those who exploit or oppress the vulnerable. The principles of Catholic social teaching, rooted in the foundational values of human dignity, solidarity, and the preferential option for the poor, echo this clarion call to action.

To truly embrace our faith, we must recognize that our spiritual growth cannot be divorced from our efforts to challenge the structures of injustice that perpetuate suffering and deprive countless human beings of their God-given dignity. The Christian spiritual journey compels us to confront uncomfortable truths about the world we inhabit, listen to the voices of people who have been silenced, and channel our beliefs into tangible actions that uplift and empower our neighbors on the margins of society.

Traditional vs. Transformative Strategies

Traditional approaches to social justice advocacy find their roots in the well-established narratives of reform and incremental progress. Forged through decades of struggle and hard-won victories, these methods are ingrained within the collective consciousness of activism, offering a sense of familiarity and reassurance. At their core, traditional approaches prioritize working within existing systems and power structures, seeking to gradually chip away at inequities and injustices through legislative reforms, policy changes, and a slow erosion of institutional barriers.

One of the hallmarks of traditional strategies is their emphasis on coalition-building and broad-based support. By aligning with diverse stakeholders, from grassroots organizations to influential political figures, these approaches aim to leverage collective strength and influence to create change from within the system. Such approaches involve a degree of compromise and strategic negotiation, as advocates navigate the intricate web of competing interests and power dynamics that govern the status quo. However, while traditional approaches have yielded tangible victories throughout history, critics argue that they ultimately perpetuate the very systems they seek to reform. By operating within the confines of existing power structures, traditional methods inherently reinforce the underlying ideologies and paradigms that gave rise to injustice in the first place. For example, Rev. Dr. Martin Luther King Jr. questioned the results of the civil rights movement because of the challenges that integration brought about. During a conversation with Harry Belafonte on the results of the civil rights struggle, Dr. King confessed, "I fear I am integrating my people into a burning house."[4] Dr. King was referring to his realization that the moral ideology of America would not uphold the nonviolent moral values that were the backbone of the civil rights movement, thus not upholding the promises that people were attempting to establish through the legislation that was being fought for. He said that now the role of the movement was not integration only but also to act as "firemen" keeping America from burning down due to the immoral laws and ideologies that caused the necessity for the civil rights movement; thus, a new approach was needed. Additionally, the incremental nature of these two strategies (coalition building and broad-based support) can be perceived as an impediment to the sweeping, systemic changes that often are necessary to challenge deeply entrenched inequities.

In contrast, transformative approaches to social justice advocacy embrace a more disruptive philosophy by rejecting the notion of working within existing systems as inherently flawed and incapable of delivering meaningful, lasting change. As we saw following the murder of George Floyd, there were many protests, boycotting, and social media campaigns that raised awareness of racial injustices, systemic and otherwise, prevalent throughout the world. These transformative approaches caused institutions to evaluate their policies and procedures and to act on changing them. This would not have happened if the protests, and other actions, had not taken place. Instead, transformative approaches seek to upend the status quo, challenging the very foundations upon which our social, political, and economic structures are built. At the heart of transformative strategies lies first a rejection of traditional power dynamics and second a commitment to amplifying the voices and experiences of our community members most directly impacted by injustice. This dual process often manifests in the form of grassroots mobilization, community-led initiatives, and the amplification of marginalized narratives.

By elevating the perspectives of people who have been historically silenced or overlooked, transformative approaches aim to redefine the very terms of the discourse, shifting power and agency to people from whom it has long been denied. Transformative approaches also offer a more holistic point of view that allows us to recognize the interconnected nature of issues such as racism, classism, gender discrimination, and environmental degradation. The result of this overarching viewpoint is an undeniable insistence that we advocate for comprehensive solutions to interlocking systems of injustice.

While transformative approaches offer a compelling vision of effective, systemic change, they have their detractors. Critics argue that these methods often lack the pragmatism and incremental progress necessary to sustain long-term momentum and tangible victories. Another point of contention is that the disruptive nature of these strategies can sometimes alienate potential allies or exacerbate existing divisions, thereby inadvertently undermining the broader pursuit of justice.

As we navigate the complexities of the traditional and transformative perspectives, it becomes clear that the path to social justice is neither linear nor one-size-fits-all. The choice between these approaches is not a binary one; it exists, rather, along a spectrum of possibilities which must be carefully navigated with nuance and intentionality. In my experience, the most effective strategy lies in a synthesis of both perspectives, where the strengths of each are leveraged to create a harmonious and adaptable framework for lasting change.

In our pursuit to establish an effective strategy for change, we must remain cognizant of the profound implications of our actions. Our decisions will not only shape the trajectories of specific campaigns and initiatives but will also be sewn into the very fabric of our society, influencing the narratives, paradigms, and collective consciousness that govern our understanding of justice, equity, and human dignity. I should tell you that I am known for having a profound appreciation of and passion for handwoven tapestries, specifically, the beadwork of my Black Masking Mardi Gras Indian culture of New Orleans, because tapestries and beadwork memorialize the unique histories of cultures lived out on the margins of society. Thus, when I talk about the fabric of our society, I'm not simply utilizing a familiar metaphor. What gets sewn into the fabric of our society really matters to me, and I think about it in literal terms. I am acutely aware that the decisions we are making have the potential to weave beauty, integrity, and dignity into the fabric of society, and we should capitalize on every opportunity to weave a lovely tapestry of life for ourselves and for future generations.

Ultimately, the pursuit of social justice is a continuous journey, one that requires a willingness to adapt, evolve, and embrace new perspectives. It is in this delicate balance, this harmonious synthesis of tradition and transformation, that we will find our way to an authentically just and equitable world. The path forward is often obscured by a maze of rhetoric and platitudes, leaving us to tackle the question of how to translate our aspirations for change into tangible, sustainable solutions. This is where we must confront harsh truths and chart a course that extends beyond mere words, embracing a commitment to action that strikes at the heart of the systemic injustices that derail lives, deaden hearts, and destroy communities.

The Scourge of Racial Injustice and Economic Oppression

At the forefront of our collective struggle lies the enduring scourge and malignant force of racial injustice, which has plagued our nation for centuries. Dubbed America's "original sin" by the United States Conference of Catholic Bishops (USCCB), racial injustice has also been the root cause of much suffering and division within our Church; in fact, it has caused the rift we see today between people in the Church and our neighbors at the margins.[5] Despite the progress made through tireless activism and hard-won victories, the specter of racism continues to cast its shadow, manifesting in insidious forms that permeate every aspect of our society. The implications of this oppression are far-reaching and devastating, from disproportionate incarceration rates that decimate families and are so destructive to communities of color, to the stark disparities in access to quality education, healthcare, and economic opportunities.

Inequities are not statistical anomalies; they are tangible manifestations of a system that has long been rigged against those who do not conform to the narrow confines of privilege and power. To confront inequities like racial injustice, we must engage in a multifaceted, concerted effort to reorganize the structures and institutions that perpetuate this injustice. This will involve everything from overhauling the criminal justice system, to implementing comprehensive policy reforms that address the systemic barriers to upward mobility within marginalized communities.

Inextricably linked with the struggle against racial injustice is the urgent need to address the pervasive economic oppression that haunts our society. The harsh realities of poverty, income inequality, and lack of access to economic opportunities create a cycle of despair that disproportionately impacts marginalized communities. Only God knows how many people are in a perpetual state of deprivation and hopelessness as a result.

Growing up in New Orleans, I saw firsthand how living in one of the poorest states in the country affects the quality of life of its residents. Without employment opportunities, many people, including the youth and families in my ministry, choose methods of making money that often lead to incarceration or death. Along with many other youth ministers from the Black and Brown communities, I have had to go above and beyond the call of our regular ministry duties to engage the youth from our communities. But brutal realities like these demand that ministry focuses on survival and self-worth rather than doing fun, enriching activities during youth group.

One of my favorite parts of the job as the youth minister of my parish happened every day at three o'clock in the afternoon, when the high schoolers would pour into my office. Humble though it was, they knew my office was a place where they were welcome, a place where they could just be. We planned events and ministry-related opportunities so that our parish, and our youth center, were safe spaces.

Another high point during the week was the Wednesday evening high school youth group get-together. It was not unusual for me or one of my adult volunteers to be waiting for these youngsters to get picked up by their parents following the event. And there was one evening in 2004 that I will never forget. I was the ride home for three students. While we were waiting outside for the parents to pick up their kids, a group of young men began making lewd comments toward the two young ladies who were with me. Immediately, I told my three students to go inside the building. The young men then started to cuss me out as they crossed the street, walking straight toward me. I told them they are welcome to come to our youth group, but I would not let anyone disrespect my students. A split-second later, one of the young men pulled out a gun and pointed it at me. I froze. My heart felt like it was pounding from outside of my chest. Before anyone could react, a police car with sirens blaring flew by on the cross street, and that was enough of an interruption to inspire the hecklers to leave. As I watched them depart, I noticed I was shaking out of fear.

Instances like these embolden me to pose tough questions to our political leaders. Why do we not have resources to engage our youth? To keep them occupied? To give them somewhere to go and something constructive to do? Why don't we have adequate employment opportunities so that men and women can take care of their families without resorting to illegal and risky activities? Why are those of us who work in the community, people like me who want to help, constantly ignored? Why are we under-resourced? And where is our Church as we navigate life on the margins?

When mechanisms that keep people from feeling safe, valued, and fulfilled are replaced with properly resourced, legitimate, effective opportunities, we create a playing field where everyone has the capacity to dream, and ultimately live out, their full God-given potential, thus creating greater change, impact, and opportunities in the world. Each little step of progress in the cycle of systemic injustice provides someone with a way out of poverty, a way into possibility.

The Catholic social teaching of solidarity reminds us that we are called to recognize that, because God is our Father, we are all brothers and sisters, and we have the responsibility—and privilege—of caring for one another. As Pope Francis wrote in *Fratelli Tutti*,

> Solidarity means much more than engaging in sporadic acts of generosity. It means thinking and acting in terms of community. It means that the lives of all are prior to the appropriation of goods by a few. It also means

> combatting the structural causes of poverty, inequality, the lack of work, land and housing, the denial of social and labour rights. It means confronting the destructive effects of the empire of money. . . . Solidarity, understood in its most profound meaning, is a way of making history, and this is what popular movements are doing.[6]

Solidarity is about much more than a fuzzy warm feeling of fellowship. It is a commitment to the phrase that concludes the Pledge of Allegiance: *With liberty and justice for all.* In other words, no one is to be left out.

Magis: A Simple Word, a Profound Call

As we explore the Catholic social teaching of solidarity, let us couple our examination with the concept of *magis*, which goes straight to the heart of Ignatian spirituality. At first glance, the word *magis* might seem unassuming, a Latin term suggesting "more" or "greater." However, within the Ignatian tradition, this word carries a profound weight, a call to embrace a life of constant self-transcendence, a relentless pursuit of excellence, and an unwavering commitment to the service of our neighbors, particularly the marginalized. In fact, the concept of *magis* is rooted in the recognition that our journey toward justice and equity is never complete, that there is always room for deeper understanding, more profound solidarity, and a more steadfast commitment to demolishing oppressive systems.

Magis is not merely a call to do more or accumulate more: rather, it is an invitation to *be* more. *Magis* summons us to cultivate a sense of empathy that is ever deeper, ever more profound. It calls us to develop a more nuanced understanding of the complexities of injustice, and to embody a more authentic and sustained commitment to our brothers and sisters who have less of a voice than we do. *Magis* is a mindset that challenges us to transcend our complacency, to push beyond our comfort zones, and to constantly reevaluate our efforts in the pursuit of a more just and equitable world.

Embracing the *magis* mindset is a lifelong journey, a continuous process of self-reflection, learning, and transformation. In our quest for a more just and equitable society, the concept of charity has long been hailed as a virtuous endeavor, and rightly so. We applaud people who donate their time, resources, or money to aid folks in need. However, as noble as these acts of kindness may be, they often fail to address the root causes of systemic injustice. Worse, they perpetuate a dynamic of inequality. What if, instead of merely alleviating the symptoms, we challenge ourselves to confront the underlying issues that create and sustain poverty, oppression, and marginalization?

Charity has its place, but its limitations must be acknowledged. While charitable efforts undoubtedly provide much-needed relief and support to our community members in immediate need, they often operate within the confines of existing systems and structures that perpetuate cycles of disadvantage. Food banks and shelters provide a temporary respite, but they do not replace the economic and social barriers with alternatives that empower the people and communities they serve. Charitable endeavors, however well-intentioned, can reinforce a dynamic of benefactor and recipient, potentially undermining the agency and dignity of people receiving aid. One example of the benefactor-recipient dynamic is when companies come into various inner-city communities to help residents create their own nonprofit organizations that are designed to meet the needs of the local community. For example, I am a proud culture bearer of New Orleans. My Black Masking Mardi Gras Indian heritage has been a part of the local community since the 1600s. Our particular group has relied on our own devices to raise the thousands of dollars that go into the materials needed to make the suits that we wear with pride on Mardi Gras and other celebrations throughout the year. However, because many of our local folks have been trained by several organizations on how to create nonprofit organizations, we have been able to obtain grant funding to aid in the purchase of the cloth, beads, feathers, needles, and so on that go into making the suits—thus allowing the funds that would have gone toward these items to go instead toward other needs of the people and families in our community. The unfortunate reality of all this is that the cultural groups, who were previously independent in their existence and decision-making, are now working at the will of these nonprofits. Thus, the culture gets watered down as entertainment for hire, where it once was a sacred, independent institution.

To address the roots of injustice, we must embrace a mindset of transformative solidarity. Transformative solidarity demands a deeper commitment to understanding the historical, political, and socioeconomic contexts that shape the experiences of marginalized communities. It calls for a collaborative, inclusive approach that amplifies the voices of our most vulnerable neighbors, thereby empowering them as active agents of change rather than passive recipients of assistance. Just as with the example of the Black Masking Mardi Gras Indian culture, empowerment occurs when the recipients are able to control their own destiny, and not be controlled by the opinions or agendas of the funders.

Ultimately, transformative solidarity calls on us to move beyond surface-level acts of charity and confront the systemic roots of injustice by inviting us to reimagine a world where equity, dignity, and justice are not mere aspirations but lived realities for everyone. The path may be arduous, but the rewards of a just, inclusive society are immeasurable. It is a journey worth making, for it is only through collective and sustained action that barriers that have divided and oppressed us can be replaced with life-affirming alternatives that will ensure a future in which the principles of transformative solidarity are woven into the fabric of our culturally diverse society.

Complementary Acts: Charity and Solidarity

The concept of *magis* serves as a guiding principle, a reminder that our work toward justice and equity is a journey of constant growth and self-transcendence. At first glance, acts of charity and practices of solidarity toward the marginalized and oppressed may appear similar: both are motivated by a desire to alleviate suffering and promote the well-being of people in need. However, upon closer examination, we discover nuances that reveal the transformative potential of solidarity to transcend the limitations of traditional charitable approaches. Charity is often understood as the voluntary giving of aid, such as money, goods, or services, to people in need. It is an act rooted in compassion and a desire to provide temporary relief from hardship. Solidarity goes a step further: it is a deeper, more enduring commitment to standing alongside the marginalized and oppressed, recognizing their inherent dignity and shared humanity. Charity can be done from a distance; solidarity is a form of accompaniment.

This comparison is significant because it highlights the fundamental differences in how we approach and address the systemic issues that perpetuate marginalization and oppression. While charity provides essential support, solidarity empowers and builds identity. Charity often operates through a top-down approach, where resources and aid are distributed from people with means to our community members in need. Solidarity, on the other hand, emphasizes a bottom-up approach that centers the voices, experiences, and agency of the marginalized communities themselves; it recognizes that true and lasting change must be driven by our neighbors who are directly affected, fostering a sense of ownership and empowerment.

Charitable acts separated from solidarity, while compassionate, can unintentionally reinforce existing power structures and dynamics. The giver holds the resources and dictates the terms of support, while the recipient is positioned as a passive beneficiary. We need to practice solidarity in order to effectively challenge these power imbalances by promoting mutual understanding, shared decision-making, and the amplification of marginalized voices. Standing in solidarity recognizes the inherent agency and dignity of people who have been oppressed and seeks to create spaces where their perspectives and experiences are valued and respected.

Charity, by its nature, often focuses on addressing immediate and short-term needs, such as providing food, shelter, or medical care. Although these efforts are crucial and lifesaving, they may fail to address the root causes of marginalization and oppression. Solidarity enables us to take a holistic, long-term approach that aspires to challenge the systemic barriers and structural inequalities that perpetuate cycles of poverty, discrimination, and disenfranchisement.

Charity can be done from a distance; solidarity is a form of accompaniment.

An effective example of this took place when we were rebuilding our youth ministries following Hurricane Katrina. The larger diocesan youth board was known as TEEN CROSS. This group was made up of high school youth from the various Catholic parishes and high schools. The reality was that there were very few representatives from our Black Catholic parishes or schools. One of the goals following the hurricane was to change this reality by having meetings between Black Catholic youth ministers and the CYO/Youth & Young Adult Ministry Office so that those in charge could hear the challenges they faced getting their youth to participate in TEEN CROSS. Following these meetings, and since we were also doing intentional outreach to the growing Hispanic youth ministry community, we had cultural sensitivity training for our volunteer coaches that worked with TEEN CROSS. Eventually we increased the number of participants from the Black Catholic community from five to more than fifty. At that point, they felt engaged and represented as part of this group of 150 youth coming from the entire archdiocese. It took intentional listening, and tough conversations about past hurts and how to share power, before the new arrivals to the group felt included and engaged. This is what the work of intentional solidarity looks like.

While charity can provide temporary relief and support to individuals, solidarity holds the potential for broader societal transformation. By challenging oppressive systems and structures, solidarity efforts can catalyze lasting change, promoting equity, justice, and the removal of systemic barriers. Solidarity fosters a sense of collective responsibility and a commitment to creating a more just and inclusive society where the rights and dignity of all individuals are respected.

The Power of Solidarity

The nuances distinguishing charity from solidarity are particularly relevant in the context of contemporary social movements and struggles for justice. From the fight against racial injustice and systemic racism to the ongoing battles for the rights of Indigenous people and environmental justice, solidarity amplifies marginalized voices, challenges oppressive structures, and creates lasting, transformative change. Movements like Black Lives Matter, for instance, have not only raised awareness about police brutality and racial injustice but have also fostered a broader solidarity movement to address the intersectional nature of oppression at the same time as it advocates for systemic reforms in areas such as education, housing, and economic opportunities. Similarly, Indigenous rights movements have embraced solidarity principles by centering the experiences and perspectives of Indigenous communities, challenging colonialism, and advocating for self-determination and the protection of ancestral lands. In our quest for a more just and equitable world, the concept of solidarity with marginalized communities has emerged as a powerful force for change. Yet, despite the noble intentions and inspiring rhetoric surrounding solidarity, genuine and impactful action remains elusive. Bridging the gaps between well-meaning words and transformative deeds is a critical challenge we must confront head-on. It is time to move beyond surface-level gestures and identify practical solutions that foster genuine solidarity, rooted in understanding, empowerment, and sustained collective action. And what better place to start than within the Body of Christ?

While the call for solidarity resonates across various social justice movements, the path to its realization is fraught with obstacles. Let's talk about these obstacles.

One primary issue is the disconnect between intention and practice. Many well-intentioned people profess their commitment to solidarity, yet their actions fall short of making a place at the table for people who have had no say in policies that directly impact them, their families, and their neighborhoods.

Another obstruction is the tendency to treat solidarity as either a one-time event or a series of isolated initiatives (as opposed to a sustained and deeply ingrained commitment). This approach lacks the long-term vision and perseverance necessary to dismantle entrenched systems of oppression and foster lasting change.

And finally, power dynamics and privilege often impede genuine solidarity efforts. People in positions of relative privilege may inadvertently perpetuate the very oppressive structures they claim to challenge. They do this by centering their own narratives and experiences rather than listening to and uplifting marginalized voices. It's like being at the dinner table and trying to share with the family a crushing situation at work, but there's one person who seizes everything you say and highjacks the conversation with "That happened to me," and "I know exactly how that feels," and "Been there, done that."

The absence of genuine solidarity hinders societal progress and fuels divisiveness.

Proposed Solutions: Actionable Steps toward Genuine Solidarity

To bridge the gaps and foster genuine solidarity where the marginalized are ignored and caused to suffer, we must embrace a multifaceted approach that addresses the various challenges head-on. Practical solutions include the six essential steps that follow.

- **Prioritizing Active Listening and Centering Marginalized Voices:** genuine solidarity begins with a willingness to listen deeply and center the experiences, perspectives, and priorities of marginalized communities. This means creating safe spaces for dialogue, amplifying the voices of the marginalized in such a way that their ideas are given equal weight to everyone else at the table, and then also actively seeking their guidance and leadership in initiatives that affect their lives.
- **Cultivating Authentic Relationships and Trust:** building genuine solidarity requires the cultivation of authentic relationships based on trust, mutual respect, and shared understanding. Solidarity is achieved through sustained engagement, open and honest communication, and a genuine commitment to learning from and supporting marginalized communities.
- **Embracing Intersectionality and Collective Liberation:** recognizing the interconnected nature of oppression is crucial to fostering genuine solidarity. By embracing intersectionality, in other words, how various forms of marginalization intersect and compound one another, we can work toward collective liberation that uplifts everyone.

- **Prioritizing Capacity Building and Resource Sharing:** solidarity efforts must prioritize the empowerment and capacity-building of marginalized communities, which involves sharing resources, providing access to education and training opportunities, and fostering economic and political self-determination. When we invest in the long-term growth and resilience of these communities, we play a part in dismantling systemic barriers and creating a more level playing field.
- **Advocating for Systemic and Policy Changes:** while grassroots initiatives are essential, genuine solidarity must also advocate for policy changes that address the root causes of marginalization and oppression. What this requires is persistent and strategic efforts to influence decision-makers and lawmakers, challenge discriminatory laws and policies, and promote the implementation of equitable and inclusive practices across all sectors of society.
- **Fostering Accountability and Continuous Learning:** genuine solidarity is an ongoing journey that requires continuous learning, self-reflection, and accountability; it is crucial to establish mechanisms for honest and constructive feedback, and to be open to acknowledging mistakes, addressing blind spots, and adapting strategies as needed. A commitment to growth and accountability ensures that solidarity efforts remain relevant, impactful, and aligned with the evolving needs of marginalized communities.

If this protocol seems too daunting to tackle, the consequences of inaction are far too grave to ignore. It is time we stand in unwavering solidarity to amplify marginalized voices and work tirelessly toward a world where the inherent dignity and rights of all individuals are upheld and celebrated. What does it mean to stand in genuine solidarity with people facing injustice and marginalization? The answer is deeply rooted in the fundamental human experience of empathy, compassion, and a shared commitment to the collective well-being of all people. In other words, we already know what an ethical human experience looks like. It looks like Jesus.

At its core, solidarity is the recognition that our individual struggles are interconnected, and that true progress can only be achieved through collective action and mutual support. We make a conscious choice to align with our community members who face systemic oppression, discrimination, and denial of their basic human rights, and we actively work toward replacing the structures that perpetuate these injustices.

Key Elements of Solidarity

In his 2015 speech to the United States Congress, Pope Francis talks about Dr. King and the importance of dreams.

> Here too I think of the march which Martin Luther King led from Selma to Montgomery fifty years ago as part of the campaign to fulfill his "dream" of full civil and political rights for African Americans.[7] That dream continues to inspire us all. I am happy that America continues to be, for many, a land of "dreams." Dreams which lead to action, to participation, to commitment. Dreams which awaken what is deepest and truest in the life of a people.[8]

To be in true solidarity, everyone must be allowed to dream; furthermore—and this part is essential—everyone must have access to a way to achieve those dreams. Herein lies the power of authentic connections, and this is why authentic solidarity with our neighbors must be a reflection of the servant-love Christ modeled, and motivate us to pray with our feet.

The following four elements are present in authentic solidarity:

- **Shared Struggle:** solidarity acknowledges that the struggles of marginalized communities are inherently intertwined, and that the fight for justice cannot be compartmentalized or siloed. We must recognize that oppression manifests in multifaceted and intersectional ways, and that true liberation requires a holistic approach toward the compounded effects of discrimination based on race, gender, class, disability, socioeconomic and employment status, education level, and other identities.
- **Amplification of Marginalized Voices:** solidarity requires a conscious effort to amplify the voices, experiences, and leadership of marginalized communities. It involves actively listening, deferring to their expertise, and creating spaces where people can articulate their needs, priorities, and visions for change without being silenced or tokenized.
- **Shared Power and Equitable Distribution of Resources:** solidarity is a tangible commitment to sharing power and resources with marginalized communities. This includes providing access to educational opportunities, economic empowerment, and decision-making

platforms, as well as advocating for policies and systemic changes that create a more equitable distribution of resources and opportunities.

- **Sustained Action:** solidarity is not a one-time event or a momentary hashtag campaign; it is a lifelong commitment to sustained action, perseverance, and resilience in the face of adversity. As such, it requires a willingness to confront resistance, backlash, and entrenched systems of oppression, while maintaining a steadfast dedication to nonviolent resistance and collective action.

Embracing solidarity in our daily lives and communities has far-reaching implications for creating a more just and equitable society, but in order to get from here to there, we must implement three different overhauls at the personal level. First, we must challenge our own biases and privileges. Second, we must seek out opportunities to amplify the voices of the marginalized. And third, we must use our most guarded resources and most precious platforms to advocate for systemic change in the following areas:

- **In the Realm of Education:** solidarity manifests through the decolonization of curricula and the inclusion of diverse perspectives and narratives, and also through the creation of inclusive learning environments that celebrate and empower marginalized students.
- **In the Workplace:** solidarity can take the forms of active allyship, advocating for equitable hiring practices, promoting diverse leadership, and challenging discriminatory policies and behaviors that perpetuate marginalization and exclusion.

- **In Our Communities:** solidarity will inspire us to engage in grassroots organizing, participate in collective action and protests, support local initiatives led by marginalized groups, and work toward creating more inclusive and welcoming spaces for all.
- **In the Realm of Disability Rights:** solidarity movements have championed the inclusion, accessibility, and equal opportunities for individuals with special needs, challenging ableist attitudes and advocating for policies and infrastructures that promote independence and participation in all aspects of society.
- **In the Global Movement for Climate Justice:** solidarity has brought together diverse communities, Indigenous peoples, and environmental advocates in a unified call for sustainable practices, environmental protection, and transition toward a more equitable and ecologically conscious future.

More than a concept or a buzzword, solidarity is a profound recognition of our shared humanity that creates a commitment to stand together, side by side, in the pursuit of justice, equity, and collective liberation. As earnest disciples of Jesus, solidarity is being actively involved in doing the work of loving our neighbor.

The power of solidarity can be witnessed in countless real-world examples where individuals and communities have come together to challenge injustice and demand transformative change. For example, in the fight against police brutality and systemic racism, we have seen formidable displays of solidarity across racial and ethnic lines, with people from diverse backgrounds standing together to demand accountability, reform, and a reimagining of public safety and community well-being.

In this instance, the power of solidarity locates itself in the capacity to transcend individual struggles and create a collective movement for transformative change. By standing together, amplifying marginalized voices, and engaging in sustained action, we can forge a path toward the heaven on earth we're supposed to be helping God create.

Throughout history, solidarity has been a powerful driving force for social change. From ancient philosophical traditions, from contemporary intersectional movements such as the civil rights, environmental, and women's liberation movements, and from the lives of saints such as St. Óscar Romero and St. Teresa of Calcutta, the evolution of solidarity has been marked by resilience, sacrifice, and an unwavering commitment to the pursuit of collective liberation. As we look to the future, the legacy of solidarity continues to inspire us to embrace our shared humanity, amplify marginalized voices, and engage in sustained action to create a more just and equitable world for all.

Practicing Solidarity in Everyday Life

Depending on where you are and what you do in your life, putting solidarity into practice may seem both intimidating and impractical. Are you a parent of school-age children? Are you a blue-collar worker? An executive? Are you an activist who isn't quite sure where to begin? Are you a member of the clergy, or involved in parish ministry? The good news is that no matter who you are or what you do, simply by making a shift in your perspective and in the way you operate, you can stand in solidarity. You can make a difference.

Following are some suggestions for how to achieve the far-reaching effects of solidarity:

- Observe the dynamics of power and privilege in your life; pay attention to who does and does not receive attention, space, and resources when decisions are made.
- Expand your knowledge and awareness of domestic and global social justice issues by taking courses, reading books and articles, and attending local talks and meetings held in public forums. Use this information to examine the ways societal structures include and exclude groups of people.
- Develop authentic relationships with marginalized groups and lean into the discomfort these relationships may cause as you gain insight into perspectives different than your own. A good place to start is to look around your own community. Find out what facilities and programs are in place for unhoused people. Are there volunteer opportunities that allow you to use your talents to help those on the margins? Are there schools in need of tutors? Does your local hospital need volunteers?
- Resist stereotypes and acknowledge the reality of oppressive histories both within and outside your communities.
- Raise awareness and educate people about social issues often left out of discussions.
- Create diverse leadership structures and pay attention to how social identities are represented and how power is structured within the organizations you are a part of.

- Provide marginalized groups space in which they can articulate how they would like to be assisted.
- Listen first, then ask how you can support and help, and then work with other people in the relevant community to accomplish the desired outcome.
- Promote and attend community events held by marginalized groups that are open to the public.

It is important to realize that change happens one person at a time, which means that getting to know one another—putting a face and a name to every story—is the starting point for everything. In a pastoral letter entitled "What We Have Seen and Heard," Black bishops discussed this concept of solidarity, saying:

> In our response to the invitation to evangelize, we as Black Catholics have before us several opportunities to assure the universal aspect of the American Church. We can do so by permitting the Catholic Church in this country to reflect the richness of African American history and its heritage. This is our contribution to the building up of the Universal Church.[9]

After being on the margins of the Church, these Black bishops were empowering their community while simultaneously advocating to their brother bishops and the wider Church that, as Sr. Thea Bowman said during her address to the USCCB, Black Catholics have gifts to share, and the Church was to stand in solidarity with this community in order to understand

and appreciate the gifts they offer.[10] This is also true when we encounter God in the margins. People who live on the periphery have gifts to give, and they are offering them to us.

Praying with Our Feet: The Catholic Social Teaching of the Dignity of Work and the Rights of Workers

The Catholic social teaching of the dignity of work and the rights of workers calls on us to protect the basic rights of all workers, including the right to engage in productive work, the right to receive fair wages, the right to own private property, and the right to organize, join unions, and pursue economic opportunity. Pope Francis reminds us in *Laudato Si´* that "we were created with a vocation to work. . . . The loss of jobs also has a negative impact on the economy 'through the progressive erosion of social capital: the network of relationships of trust, dependability, and respect for rules, all of which are indispensable for any form of civil coexistence.'"[11] The current advocacy position of the USCCB tells us that "the most effective way to build a just economy is to make decent work at decent wages available for all those capable of working."[12]

One of the first things people ask when they meet someone is *What do you do?* The reality is that we are defined by our work, and in a capitalistic society we need to work to survive. For many, work is our identity. Personally, my nickname back home is "Preach" because I am usually the "church person" in social or community settings. Ministry is not only my way of paying my bills, it is also my way of serving in God's creation. This is how the economy should function—it should create tangible ways for people to use their God-given gifts to build a better society. Humanity, not profit margins, should be at the forefront of all economic decisions.

As Pope Francis states in *Evangelii Gaudium*:

> Growth in justice requires more than economic growth, while presupposing such growth; it requires decisions, programs, mechanisms and processes specifically geared to a better distribution of income, the creation of sources of employment, and an integral promotion of the poor which goes beyond a simple welfare mentality. I am far from proposing an irresponsible populism, but the economy can no longer turn to remedies that are a new poison, such as attempting to increase profits by reducing the work force, thereby adding to the ranks of the excluded.[13]

Where are we as a society on this? The majority of poor people suffer so that the few at the top can prosper. Intricately connected to the struggle against racial injustice is the urgent need to address the pervasive economic oppression that plagues our society. The harsh realities of poverty, income inequality, and lack of access to economic opportunities have created a cycle of despair that disproportionately impacts marginalized communities, trapping countless human beings in a state of perpetual deprivation and hopelessness.

Workers' rights, fair wages, and safe working conditions are inextricably linked to issues of poverty, access to education, and the broader socioeconomic landscape. Addressing economic injustice means confronting the root causes of income inequality, challenging corporate greed, and advocating for policies that promote financial inclusion and socioeconomic mobility. For instance, investing in quality education and providing equal access to educational opportunities not only combats racial and socioeconomic disparities, it also empowers us to challenge gender norms, advocate for workers' rights, and promote environmental stewardship. Education serves as a powerful catalyst for personal growth, critical thinking, and the cultivation of a more inclusive and just society. Similarly, promoting economic empowerment and financial inclusion can break the cycles of poverty and dismantle the systemic barriers that perpetuate injustice. By providing access to financial resources, entrepreneurial opportunities, and fair wages, people can gain greater control over their lives, challenge oppressive structures, and invest in the well-being of their communities.

As we preach about a just society and the dignity of humans within the walls of our church, it is up to all of us to pray with our feet. To step out. To create the conditions where justice—especially for our community members who do not have the platform to speak for themselves—is within reach.

Practicing the Dignity of Work and Workers' Rights in Everyday Life

In a world where work is a means to survival, we must make sure that every worker is respected and treated fairly. We must look at how the concept of work helps people live out their true role as people made in the image and likeness of God. To operate so that this can happen, companies must put people above profits. This is why Pope Francis has challenged the concept of capitalism. We must create a society that looks at the concept of work as something that benefits humans in terms of their purpose, their dreams, and how they interact with the world. Unfortunately, as a consequence of the reality of working in today's society, too many people on the margins are too easily exploited.

It is important to live out our faith lives in our everyday choices and encounters. This is how we pray with our feet. It is also one of the most important ways we give witness to our values. Here are some practical ways we can practice the principle of the dignity of work and workers' rights:

- Research how companies treat and value the people they employ. If their behavior isn't in alignment with your principles, express yourself with your dollars by not buying their services or products.
- Encourage political leaders to promote policies that support the rights of workers over the profits of institutions. And then make sure you go to the polls and vote according to your principles.
- Research, and educate your community, on how companies can support workers beyond providing a living wage.
- Connect with people in marginalized communities to educate them about financial management, investment, and how to provide economic opportunities within their community. Maybe you can do something as basic as help people write a resumé; maybe you can help someone get a job by recommending them to vendors or service providers you use.
- In your community, learn about the challenges workers face, and lend your own talents and abilities to help them overcome those challenges.

- Connect with local nonprofits and financial institutions to create pathways to fulfilling employment for the community, especially for the youth and young adults who live in marginalized communities.
- Make sure you are investing your money in ethically sound companies.

No matter what a person's profession might be, everyone should feel empowered and proud of the work that they are doing. We are all contributors to the flow of society, and our work ideally should add to the process of making the world a better place for everyone.

CHAPTER 2

SHOWING UP SO GOD CAN SHOW OUT

As the spiritual journey continues and deepens, our "sight" is transformed, and we begin to "see the light." We become illumined as if someone turned on a light switch revealing something that had been there all along but was, until that moment, unseen. Again, hearkening back to the song "Amazing Grace," we can't help but relate to the lyrics "I once was lost, but now I'm found/Was blind, but now I see." In the Spiritual Exercises of St. Ignatius, the focus of the second week is on *illumination*. We are invited to contemplate Jesus in the Gospels and make a choice to follow him—or, as I like to say, "show up so he can show out."

In my twenty-five-plus years of full-time ministry, God has had me show up so he can show out in various spaces and places. The blessings have been many: I have witnessed young people see their worth and take their place in leadership in the Church and community; I have witnessed community healing after violent events between groups in that community; and I have seen groups fight with unwavering tenacity and hope to end oppressive conditions, eventually achieving whatever social justice issue they were striving to accomplish.

Of all the ministries I've participated in, my favorite is working with people who have been incarcerated. New Orleans, unfortunately, is the mass incarceration capital of the world. The reality of a poor economy, failing schools, lack of opportunities, and the for-profit prison system have exacerbated the over-incarceration crisis. Even during my work as a youth minister early in my career, much of my time was devoted to ministering to the young people and their families affected by the United States prison industrial complex. There is no doubt in my mind that this is pro-life work.

Eventually, I began to lead retreats at some of the prisons in South Louisiana. The men and women I met were hungry for the faith. I quickly learned it was not simply my presence that inspired and encouraged them; they too were doing the same for me. In fact, no matter how many times my profession necessitates moving from one place to another, I keep a stack of notecards with me that never fail to inspire me. These are the notecards on which prisoners answered the question of where they see God at work in their lives. Many of these people no longer have anyone on the outside connecting with them; understandably, then, they feel forgotten, purposeless, and discarded by society. What I find astonishing is that these folks should feel hopeless, and yet they have hope. They sing louder than any group I have been with when it is time for praise and worship. They are proud of their faith, and they openly evangelize other prisoners to witness for Christ in those spaces.

They give me hope.

During one the hardest times of my life, God spoke to me through these people living behind razor wire. I moved to New York after getting engaged, sacrificing everything to make the relationship work. Ultimately, I called off the engagement due to various issues that my fiancée and I could not work out. Afterward, I was devastated, lonely, and depressed. Some of my local church members from Harlem and Brooklyn would check in on me, but I was still upset. I could not wait until August when I would be moving back home to New Orleans and start over.

One day I received an unexpected notice that I had a package in the mail room. After unpacking the box, I pulled out a crystal cross that was engraved with the message *In appreciation for your service in God's work.* Also enclosed was a greeting card that simply said, "We miss you, Preach! We hope you are ok and love you." The card was signed, "Your brothers from the Catholic Community at Rayburn Correctional Center."

The tears flowed.

God was speaking to me through these men who had chosen to trust me. The result? Two-way relationships in which both sides of the razor wire were served. As for God, I saw in their heartfelt gift and card that he was telling me to trust him. To know that God was still with me, despite the painful ending of an important relationship, showed me there were better days ahead.

And more work to do.

I could not wait to get back home and visit my friends behind bars. The first retreat I conducted back there was oxymoronic: it was simultaneously tearful and cheerful. We joked, laughed, and shared love. Out in the real world, some of the men may not interact due to different racial or socioeconomic makeup, but in there, we all were family. One of the things I love about these men is the way they share a zeal for following Christ. It's contagious. Despite their circumstances, these prisoners share love and hope. They know that despite what is going in their lives, no matter their condition, true freedom and hope is found in doing God's work. They witness to one another about how they can resist evil in prison, and also how they can encourage other people to do the same.

Through these relationships with men very definitely living on the perimeter of society, I was able to know Christ's love for me. I never expected that I would be healed by people who appear to be so broken, so wounded, so desperately lacking in some of the most basic of human rights. No, I never dreamed that they would help me heal. But they did.

Embodying the Examen Prayer to Confront Systemic Injustices

The men and women I encountered in prisons are shining examples of how to live out the Examen prayer of St. Ignatius. This prayer invites us to reflect on our day in order to recognize how, when, and in what ways God has been present to us. How these prisoners live life embodies the steps of the Examen in these ways:

- they continue to give thanks despite their situation;
- they witness to where God has shown up and shown out in their day;
- they reflect on their decisions, good and bad, and how these decisions affect their relationship with God and his creation; and
- they seek forgiveness and make a vow to strive for change wherever they fall short.

To me, men and women who live outside of society and yet still feel very much the pull of family and home are sources of inspiration. When I am with them, it is as if they "wash my feet." When I leave their spaces, it is as if I carry their confidence in Christ with me, and I cannot help but be freshly motivated to continue battling injustice. This is how I strive to live like Christ.

Despite much progress, systemic injustices and oppressive structures continue to persist, presenting ongoing challenges in the pursuit of a beloved community. There is something reverential about the beloved community we call "home." Surprisingly, I saw how reverence acts like a glue that prevents people from falling apart in the prison system. Now, don't get me wrong—prison is a brutally tough place in which to live. And yet, pods of peace and kindness appear like oases in the desert of prison deprivation, and these become the beloved communities that sustain souls.

The journey toward a beloved community must acknowledge and address the collective trauma experienced by marginalized and oppressed communities as a result of systemic injustices, violence, and ongoing forms of oppression. Honoring and healing collective trauma involves creating safe spaces for storytelling, collective processing, and the validation of shared experiences. It requires culturally responsive and trauma-informed practices that promote emotional safety, trust, and a recognition of the ongoing impacts of trauma on individuals, families, and entire communities.

The healing of collective trauma happens when we heal the people who have been traumatized. And how do we do that? We do it by embracing traditional healing modalities, engaging in rituals and ceremonies that honor the resilience and strength of communities, and fostering a sense of collective resilience and post-traumatic growth. By acknowledging and addressing collective trauma, communities can begin to heal deep wounds, reclaim their narratives, and cultivate a sense of empowerment and hope for a future rooted in justice and wholeness. We need only look at the lives of Jesus's beloved disciples and how they handled the collective traumas of their ministry. Following the crucifixion of their leader, and what their brothers and sisters in the faith experienced, they had to manage how to persevere in the midst of persecution by refusing to relinquish their narrative. They did not forsake Christ. They practiced the *magis* even before it had been named. This is what all of us must do. We must keep our eyes on the goal of reclaiming our beloved communities, and on the goal of healing our beloved people from collective and individual trauma. And we must do more. And we must do better.

Building Intergenerational Bridges

The creation of a beloved community is a multigenerational project, where young and old and everyone in between can share their wisdom, learn from one another's experiences, and aspire to co-create solutions to the problems that grow the generation gap and divide us as a community. To say it another way, community involves honoring the knowledge and lived experiences of elders; providing mentorship and guidance to younger generations; and creating opportunities for intergenerational dialogue, knowledge exchange, and collaborative action. And it also involves *empowering* the youth as agents of change, *amplifying* their voices, and *supporting* their leadership as they shape the future. By building intergenerational bridges, communities tap into a rich tapestry of perspectives, foster a sense of continuity and shared purpose, and ensure that the legacy of struggle, resilience, and hope is carried forward through the generations.

As we grapple with the enormity of systemic challenges, it is imperative that we move beyond the realm of rhetoric and theory and embrace a commitment to tangible, sustainable action. On the grassroots level, we must empower and support community-led initiatives to address the immediate needs of marginalized populations. From establishing community resource centers and support networks to organizing educational workshops and advocacy campaigns, localized efforts can have a profound impact on fostering resilience, empowerment, and collective action.

An example of this kind of praying with our feet is the Black Catholic Young Adult Initiative. With the support of the Black and Indian Mission Office, the Knights of Peter Claver Foundation, the Catholic Campaign for Human Development, and other entities, a group of Black Catholic young adults (ranging from eighteen to forty years of age) were gathered from around the country at Xavier University of Louisiana—the only Catholic historically Black college or university (HBCU) in the country—to have an honest discussion about why their generation is struggling to connect with the Church and what can be done about it. This demographic is difficult to engage because there are limited connections due to their exodus from the Church for reasons mentioned earlier; when national programs take place, this is the most underrepresented group. The gathering was characterized by intense discussions between Black Catholic young adults of many different demographics—single, married, students, parents, disaffiliated in the Church, and full-time employed ministers. A report entitled "Black Catholic Young Adult Recommendations from the Gathering at Xavier University of Louisiana 11/16/2023–11/19/2023"[14] summarizes the fruits of the proceedings. The report also includes observations and recommendations about what is needed from the Church and from the Black Catholic community in order to heal wounds and bridge gaps. Presented in conjunction with webinars and presentations, the document was seen as revolutionary because it was one of the few times the Church heard from a demographic that feels apathetic about the relevance of the Church in their lives.

We must also engage in concerted policy and advocacy efforts, leveraging our collective voices and influence to drive systemic change at the legislative and institutional levels. Strategies may involve lobbying for comprehensive policy reforms, advocating for increased funding and resource allocation, and holding elected officials and decision-makers accountable for addressing the pressing issues of injustice and inequity. Furthermore, we must cultivate strategic partnerships with diverse stakeholders, including government agencies, private sector entities, and influential community leaders. By leveraging the collective resources, expertise, and reach of these entities, we can amplify our efforts and create a unified front in the pursuit of sustainable solutions. I believe that this has been why my ministry over the years has been effective.

No matter where I go, I am excited to connect with the Christ who is already there, even if he shows up in a form that I am unfamiliar with. Every encounter is an opportunity to experience God's love, and to share it as well.

Sustaining the Momentum: Building Resilient Movements

Effecting lasting change is not a sprint; it is a marathon that requires unwavering dedication, perseverance, and a commitment to sustained action. To ensure the longevity and impact of our efforts, we must prioritize the cultivation of resilient and self-sustaining movements that can withstand the inevitable challenges and setbacks that will arise along the way. This involves fostering a culture of leadership development and succession planning, empowering a new generation of activists and advocates to carry the torch of social justice forward. When we invest in comprehensive training programs, mentorship initiatives, and capacity-building efforts, we ensure that our movements are fortified with the knowledge, skills, and resources necessary to navigate the complex terrain of systemic change.

> Each church parish, in every aspect of its ministry and educational programs, up and down and across all levels of administration, has the perfect setup to begin enacting all the strategies and dynamics I've been talking about throughout the book. This is where it can all begin.

Additionally, we must prioritize self-care and community support systems, recognizing the emotional and psychological toll this work takes on community advocates at the forefront of the struggle. Once we start creating spaces for healing, reflection, and collective care, we will also cultivate a sense of resilience to weather the storms that inevitably lie ahead, and one of the likeliest spaces where we can begin to nurture all this healing is at the parish level. Each church parish, in every aspect of its ministry and educational programs, up and down and across all levels of administration, has the perfect setup to begin enacting all the strategies and dynamics I've been talking about throughout the book. This is where it can all begin. This is where it should begin—in embracing the audacity of hope.

Confronted with seemingly insurmountable challenges and deeply entrenched systems of oppression, it can be tempting to succumb to despair and resignation. Yet, it is in these moments of adversity when we must redouble our resolve and embrace, as Barack Obama writes about in his book of the same title, the audacity of hope.[15] As we navigate the complexities of systemic injustice, let us be guided by the words of elders and ancestors who have paved the way before us, all of them courageous community members who dared to dream of a better future and then tirelessly fought to make that dream a reality. From the unwavering courage of women's suffragists and civil rights icons to the resilience of grassroots activists, their legacy serves as a beacon of inspiration, reminding us that lasting change is not only possible but inevitable when we remain steadfast in our commitment to justice.

Humility: The Heartbeat of Justice and Mercy

Humility is the heartbeat of justice and mercy. In the pursuit of a more equitable world, humility stands out as a transformative force, a wellspring from which true understanding and reconciliation flow. Humility is the antidote to the arrogance that fuels oppression and injustice. It requires a willingness to set aside preconceptions, listen with an open heart, and acknowledge the inherent worth and dignity of all human beings. Humility recognizes that our perspectives are limited, our biases deeply ingrained, and our knowledge incomplete. It beckons us to walk the path of lifelong learning, embracing the wisdom found in diverse experiences and cultures.

At its core, humility is the foundation upon which empathy and compassion are built. With humility, we shed the blinders of privilege and confront the harsh realities faced by people whose voices have been silenced or disregarded. Only through this process of humble introspection can we begin to rectify the structures that have perpetuated injustice for far too long. It is not easy to fully articulate what humility is, but we all can recognize it when we are in its presence. It is powerful when humility makes its presence known in our discussions and meetings. We must remember that life is not about us; it's about what God does through us. And it is in humility where we create room to experience his majesty.

The etymology of the word *humility* traces back to the Latin *humus*, meaning *earth* or *ground*. Thus, the word serves as a reminder that we are all formed from the same soil, interconnected and interdependent. Humility is not weakness; it is the courageous act of relinquishing the ego's desire for dominance and control, and it requires that we acknowledge our limitations, biases, and capacity to harm, even if we possess the best of intentions. In the context of social transformation, humility plays a pivotal role in fostering reconciliation and healing as it establishes the necessary space for dialogue, understanding, and the acknowledgment of past wrongs.

Without humility, efforts toward justice and mercy become tainted by arrogance and self-righteousness, perpetuating cycles of resentment and resistance. Humility, on the other hand, paves the way for truth-telling, accountability, and genuine reconciliation, where both oppressor and oppressed can find common ground and work together toward a more just and equitable future. As such, humility is not only an individual virtue. When it permeates the fabric of our institutions, organizations, and systems, humility calls for a paradigm shift, where power and decision-making are decentralized, and the voices of those who have been marginalized are amplified and valued.

Here are some actionable steps we can take to embody the approach of humility:

- Engage in ongoing self-reflection and personal growth, actively challenging our own biases, prejudices, and assumptions.
- Seek out resources, workshops, and educational opportunities to foster greater self-awareness and cultural competence.
- Cultivate active listening skills and create spaces for open and respectful dialogue, where diverse perspectives can be shared and understood without judgment or confrontation.
- Support and participate in community-based initiatives that address issues of injustice, marginalization, and systemic inequality. Contribute time, resources, and expertise to amplify the voices and efforts of grassroots movements.
- Advocate for policy reform and legislative action that promotes equity, human rights, and restorative justice principles. Engage in advocacy efforts at local, state, and national levels, holding elected officials accountable and demanding progressive change.

- Embrace restorative practices in our daily lives, workplaces, educational settings, and communities. Seek to resolve conflicts through dialogue, understanding, and a focus on healing and growth, rather than punishment or alienation.
- Lead by example, embodying the principles of justice, mercy, and humility in our interactions and relationships. Demonstrate a willingness to learn, evolve, and acknowledge our own shortcomings and blind spots.
- Where is the Church in all of these efforts? Say so explicitly. If you're too shy to tackle state or federal legislatures, start with your local parish. See what I'm saying? Keep bringing it back to Jesus. Back to being Catholic. Back to being a disciple of Jesus.

By embracing these actions, we can ignite a flame of transformation within ourselves and our communities, sparking a movement that transcends boundaries and inspires lasting, systemic change. Through our collective efforts, we can create a world where justice and mercy are not merely aspirations but lived realities.

Standing on the Shoulders of Those Who Strived for Justice

As we stand on the shoulders of courageous ancestors who came before us and reflect on the triumphs of past social justice movements, we are reminded of the immense power that resides within each individual voice and in the collective strength of unified action. Whether it's advocating for racial justice, combating climate change, protecting the rights of marginalized communities, or fighting against forms of oppression, our individual and collective actions have the power to shape a more just and equitable world. Let us embrace the courage to raise our voices, to listen and learn from diverse experiences, and to join forces in collective action.

From the depths of our collective consciousness emerges a pair of questions that pierce the veil of complacency and ignite a fire within our souls: Can we, as a global community, transcend the boundaries of the status quo and dare to envision a world reshaped by the transformative principles of Catholic social teaching and Ignatian spirituality? Can we muster the courage and conviction to confront the injustices that plague our societies, and forge a path toward a more just, equitable, and compassionate existence?

These questions strike at the very core of our human experience, for they challenge us to confront the harsh realities that have become all too familiar—poverty, oppression, discrimination, and the exploitation of our planet's finite resources. It is demanded that we rise above the complacency that has become a comfortable cloak, shielding us from the hard truths and difficult decisions that true transformation requires.

Within these daunting queries lie the seeds of hope—the promise of a world where the inherent dignity of every human being is honored, where the pursuit of the common good supersedes individual self-interest, and where the call to live in solidarity with one another echoes through every action and decision we make.

Some argue that the ideals of Catholic social teaching and Ignatian spirituality are noble but impractical, unable to withstand the harsh realities of a world driven by greed, power, and self-interest. Many contend that true transformation can only be achieved through top-down, centralized efforts, dismissing the power of grassroots movements and community-driven initiatives. Yet, there is a unique approach, a path forged by the intersection of faith and action, that offers the promise of a transformed world. It is an approach rooted in the profound wisdom of Catholic social teaching, which calls us to uphold the inherent dignity of every human being, to pursue the common good, and to live in solidarity with one another. It is an approach illuminated by the principles of Ignatian spirituality, which invites us to find God in all things, to embrace a spirit of discernment, and to act with a deep sense of purpose and intention.

Can we, as a global community, transcend the boundaries of the status quo and dare to envision a world reshaped by the transformative principles of Catholic social teaching and Ignatian spirituality?

Praying with Our Feet: The Catholic Social Teaching of Option for the Poor and Vulnerable

The Catholic social teaching of option for the poor and vulnerable reminds us that we are called to pay special attention to the needs of people who are poor and vulnerable. It has been said that the moral test for a society is how that society treats its most vulnerable members. The *Catechism of the Catholic Church* teaches us that:

> The Church's love for the poor . . . is a part of her constant tradition. This love is inspired by the Gospel of the Beatitudes, of the poverty of Jesus, and of his concern for the poor. . . . Those who are oppressed by poverty

> are the object of a preferential love on the part of the Church which, since her origin and in spite of the failings of many of her members, has not ceased to work for their relief, defense, and liberation.[16]

To have a preferential option for the poor and vulnerable means to place the needs of our neighbors who are poor and most vulnerable before all others. Jesus made it clear that the poor and vulnerable have a special place in God's kingdom, and he taught that when we tend to the needs of community members who are poor and vulnerable, we are looking after him.

Grasping the true nature and depth of poverty is essential to our efforts in social justice advocacy. The following terms and concepts that surround this issue serve as a foundation for our understanding, guiding us toward effective and meaningful action:

- **Poverty:** this word is often tossed around, yet its true weight and implications remain elusive. We may envision images of hunger and destitution, but poverty is a multifaceted phenomenon that extends far beyond material deprivation. It is a relentless cycle of disadvantage, a systemic erosion of human dignity and potential.
- **Absolute Poverty:** this term refers to the most extreme and dehumanizing form of poverty, defined by a lack of access to basic human needs such as food, clean water, shelter, and healthcare. It is a stark reality for millions around the world, where survival itself is a daily struggle. Absolute poverty is not just a matter of statistics; it is a crushing burden that strips individuals of their fundamental rights and opportunities for self-determination.

- **Relative Poverty:** in contrast to absolute poverty, relative poverty is measured against the standard of living in a particular society. It refers to the inability to afford an adequate standard of living, as determined by the economic and social norms of a community. This form of poverty can manifest in various ways, such as lack of access to quality education, healthcare, or housing, even in affluent nations. Relative poverty is a sobering reminder that poverty is not merely a matter of material deprivation but a complex interplay of societal factors and systemic inequalities.
- **Structural Poverty:** at the heart of the poverty crisis lies a network of deeply entrenched social, economic, and political systems that perpetuate and reinforce disadvantage. Structural poverty refers to the barriers and obstacles that prevent individuals and communities from escaping the cycle of poverty, despite their best efforts. These structures may include discriminatory policies, lack of access to opportunities, or institutional biases that favor the privileged. One example is the discrimination that many people of color have experienced when trying to purchase a home, especially in a neighborhood where people of color are nonexistent or the minority. The desire to "climb" the economic ladder is faced with unique hurdles for those on the margins. Addressing structural poverty requires a holistic approach that challenges and dismantles these oppressive systems.
- **Intergenerational Poverty:** for far too many, poverty is not a temporary state but a multigenerational reality. Intergenerational poverty is the brutal transfer of

economic and social disadvantages from one generation to the next, creating a vicious cycle of deprivation and marginalization. Children born into poverty face immense challenges, from limited access to quality education and healthcare, to the psychological burdens of living in scarcity. Breaking this cycle demands a comprehensive approach that addresses not only material needs but also the underlying socioeconomic and cultural factors that perpetuate this cycle.

- **Poverty of Opportunity:** while poverty is often associated with material deprivation, it also encompasses a deeply rooted lack of access to opportunities. Poverty of opportunity refers to the systemic barriers that prevent individuals and communities from realizing their full potential, whether through inadequate education, limited job prospects, or restricted social mobility. It is a form of poverty that stifles human potential and undermines the fundamental principles of equity and justice.

As we move forward in our exploration of the multifaceted dimensions of poverty, these defined terms will serve as guideposts, illuminating the complexities and nuances of this global crisis. By fostering a deeper understanding of poverty's many facets, we can develop more empathetic and effective strategies for addressing its root causes and promoting lasting change. True social justice is a collective endeavor, one that requires us to stand shoulder-to-shoulder with community advocates fighting for their dignity, their rights, and their chance to thrive. It is a challenge to shed our preconceptions, to listen with open hearts and minds, and to be willing partners in the ongoing struggle for a more just and equitable world.

Privilege and Poverty in Society

In the tapestry of our society, two distinct and contrasting threads are woven to create a striking dichotomy. On one side, we find the affluence and ease of privilege, where opportunities abound and comfort is a given. On the other, the harsh realities of poverty persist. This casts a long shadow of deprivation, marginalization, and limited choices. To fully grasp the contrasts between privilege and poverty—and to address the systemic barriers that perpetuate these divides—we must examine several critical aspects of human experience that form the fundamental building blocks of a dignified and fulfilling life: access to education, healthcare, housing, and employment.

In the tapestry of our society, two distinct and contrasting threads are woven to create a striking dichotomy. On one side, we find the affluence and ease of privilege, where opportunities abound and comfort is a given. On the other, the harsh realities of poverty persist.

Now, let us initiate a difficult conversation about the psychological and emotional implications of these disparities, as well as the insupportable perpetuation of generational cycles that entrench poverty. For people born into privilege, the world is brimming with boundless opportunities and resources. Quality education is a given, paving the way for future success and personal growth. Access to healthcare is unquestioned, ensuring that physical and mental well-being are prioritized. Safe and comfortable housing provides a nurturing environment for development, while a multitude of employment prospects offers financial stability and self-actualization.

In stark contrast, the path for our neighbors mired in poverty is fraught with obstacles at every turn. Educational opportunities are often limited, hampering intellectual growth and perpetuating cycles of underachievement. Healthcare is a luxury, with preventable illnesses and chronic conditions left untreated, eroding both physical and mental health. Substandard housing conditions, coupled with food insecurity and exposure to environmental hazards, create a toxic environment that stifles human potential.

In addition to material deprivations, the psychological and emotional toll of poverty is also profound and far-reaching. Constant stress, anxiety, and feelings of hopelessness become all-consuming, eroding self-worth and perpetuating a sense of powerlessness. This emotional burden often manifests in increased rates of mental health issues, substance abuse, and strained interpersonal relationships. In contrast, the privilege of financial security and access to resources fosters a sense of confidence, resilience, and emotional well-being as the freedom to pursue personal growth, explore interests, and engage in enriching activities contributes to a more balanced and fulfilling life.

As we confront the stark contrasts between privilege and poverty, it becomes evident that socioeconomic disparities are not mere coincidences but rather the result of deeply entrenched systems of oppression and marginalization. Oppressive systems, rooted in historical injustices, perpetuate inequality and deprive individuals, families, indeed entire communities of their fundamental human rights and dignity. To address such disparities, we must challenge the structures, policies, and mindsets that enable and sustain inequity. We must call to action all those in positions of privilege to use their influence and resources to dismantle oppressive systems and establish pathways for equitable access to education, healthcare, housing, and economic opportunities.

In the journey toward social justice, the role of allies and advocates is paramount. When people in power join their neighbors in need, the fruit of their efforts can be seen in community-led initiatives and partnerships with grassroots organizations, and in the utilizing of platforms, mainly those allowing networking and access to resources and visibility that would normally be unattainable without these alliances, to raise awareness and effect change. Fostering allyship involves a genuine commitment to self-education, active listening, and a willingness to cede space and power when necessary. Allies working side-by-side in collaborative efforts empower and uplift by serving with humility, empathy, and the recognition that true progress must sidestep old paternalistic attitudes and approaches.

As we reflect on the stark contrasts between privilege and poverty, we are confronted with a choice to perpetuate the status quo or to embrace a path toward genuine and lasting change. The journey ahead is not an easy one, but it is a necessary one. An urgent one. By acknowledging and challenging the systems that perpetuate inequality, by fostering allyship and amplifying the voices of the marginalized, and by embracing our shared humanity, we can forge a future where privilege and poverty are no longer opposing realities. In this way we will be working to create a mode of life on earth that is more in keeping with the Beatitudes.

Practicing an Option for the Poor and Vulnerable in Everyday Life

We must remember that God calls all of us to share our gifts with our brothers and sisters on the margins. The poor are most vulnerable and also most in need, yet they are the most invisible to society. Scripture reminds us, "Truly I tell you, just as you did it to one of the least of these who are members of my family, you did it to me" (Matthew 25:40). The point, though, is not to do these things to make ourselves feel good. The point is to connect with people outside our usual circle and do what we can to empower them and help them connect with Christ who is already present in their midst. The following are some suggestions for ways to connect with sincerity and authenticity:

- To live out God's love, we must take action. Analyze how your community treats the poor and vulnerable. You can analyze the needs of the community by looking at city budgets and how local demographics are served by agencies that address the needs of marginalized people. See what actions should be taken to ensure that the needs of these people are addressed.
- Make sure groups that serve the poor and vulnerable—for example Catholic Charities, community food banks, grassroots groups, and local nonprofits—are advocated for when budget and resource decisions are made within your community.
- Educate your local organizations, especially Catholic parishes and schools, about the need for all of us to serve the poor and vulnerable, and then do what you can to assist in creating opportunities for these people.
- Make sure any assistance given is holistic, which means that the service offered is directed toward the physical, emotional, and spiritual needs of the poor and vulnerable in your communities.
- Address material poverty by paying attention to the realities of the living conditions that need to be improved, including your local school systems, the ways that crime affects the families and children in your community, the effects of mass incarceration on those

families, the reality of sexual exploitation of the most vulnerable of the vulnerable, and the crippling effects of unemployment and lack of healthcare. Research and work with community organizations that are already doing what they can to address these issues.

- Confront moral poverty by challenging each and every structure that denies the primacy of the human person. In this era of profit over ethics, advocate for policies and structures that refuse to, and do not, exploit the poor and vulnerable.
- Be a positive force in remedying spiritual poverty by having the courage to be a witness of Christ's love in the public square and, at the same time, be courageous in not shying away from challenging conversations as you advocate for the poor and vulnerable.
- *Do not* have a savior mentality when engaging with the poor and vulnerable. Rather, view these people as equals, people who, just like you, are made in the image and likeness of God.

Take time to work with the marginalized. There is no program, no matter how well-designed or well-intentioned, that can take the place of one-to-one relationships. This is exactly how Christ walked among the poor of his time. He did not hold himself above anyone; he met them where they were, and he lovingly encountered them as family. Let us learn from Jesus how we can learn from each other. Just as Christ walked among the marginalized, we too must do the same, and in a

Let us learn from Jesus how we can learn from each other. Just as Christ walked among the marginalized, we too must do the same, and in a loving way, to be true disciples.

loving way, to be true disciples. The key point to remember in this countercultural vision of faith in action is to lead with love, and then make sure we are not viewing charitable works as transactional.

Praying with Our Feet: The Catholic Social Teaching of the Dignity of the Human Person

The Catholic social teaching of the dignity of the human person calls us to ask whether our actions as a society respect or threaten the life and dignity of each human being. In other words, the way we respond to the needs of people has everything to do with recognizing the presence of Jesus within them. This begins by recognizing the inherent, God-given dignity of every single human being. Human dignity is at the very heart of Catholic morality because every human being has value as a child of God.

Poverty is not defined simply by a lack of material resources and financial constraints, but also by the absence of dignity, opportunity, and hope. The essence of what it means to live in poverty involves a reality that touches the heart of human experience. To understand the crux of poverty, we must reframe our perspective through the lens of human dignity.

At its core, human dignity is the intrinsic value and inherent worth bestowed upon every human being, regardless of their socioeconomic status, race, gender, or any other defining characteristic. It is a fundamental human right that should be recognized, respected, and upheld for all. Sadly, the harsh realities of poverty strip individuals of this inherent dignity, relegating them to lives marked by marginalization, stigma, and disempowerment.

Poverty is often perceived as a personal failing—a consequence of laziness or lack of ambition. This misconception has perpetuated harmful stereotypes and biases, further entrenching stigmas surrounding people living in poverty. The truth is that poverty is a multifaceted issue with deep-rooted systemic causes, and it's almost always beyond the control of the person immersed in it. It is the manifestation of societal imbalances, inadequate access to resources, and structural barriers that impede economic mobility and social inclusion. Poverty is not a choice; it's a circumstance.

Upholding human dignity in the face of poverty requires a radical shift in our collective mindset. We must acknowledge the inherent worth of every human being and reject the stigma and marginalization that have long troubled our neighbors living in poverty. By recognizing their resilience, strength, and unique perspectives, we can create a more inclusive and just society that empowers and uplifts all. And then we have to ask ourselves: what can we do to help those on the margins?

The preferential option for the poor—a principle deeply rooted in faith and social justice movements—calls us to prioritize the needs and voices of people experiencing poverty while also urging us to seek out and amplify their perspectives. In so doing, we ensure that the poor are not merely passive recipients of aid but active agents in shaping solutions and driving positive change. This commitment to centering the experiences of the poor is not an act of charity but a moral imperative rooted in the belief that every human being deserves to live with dignity and opportunity.

Championing human dignity in the context of poverty requires a multifaceted approach that addresses both immediate needs and long-term systemic changes; as such, it involves providing access to essential resources such as food, shelter, healthcare, and education while simultaneously undoing the structural barriers that perpetuate cycles of poverty. A holistic approach empowers individuals and communities, enabling them to break free from the shackles of deprivation to achieve their full potential.

In the pursuit of human dignity and justice, we must embrace the power of collaboration and partnership. We must work alongside our community members affected by poverty, fostering open dialogue and co-creating solutions rooted in their lived experiences and aspirations. Moreover, we must recognize that poverty is not an isolated issue but one that intersects with other forms of marginalization and oppression. Issues of race, gender, disability, and other identities often compound the challenges faced by our neighbors living in poverty. Addressing these intersectional complexities requires a nuanced understanding and a commitment to fostering inclusivity and equity across all spectrums of society.

Here are some ways of practicing the dignity of being human in everyday life:

- See the world through the eyes of people who are different from you. Understand that your perception and experience of life is not the only reality.
- When engaging with various communities, especially marginalized groups, listen more than you speak, so that you can learn what the real needs are. This shows that you value their partnership in addressing whatever issue is being discussed.
- Respect a group's social norms. Understand that the way you might normally do or say things might not be acceptable, or may even be offensive, to certain groups. Learn from the group as you engage with them.

- Be inclusive by inviting people to be a part of the discussion and problem-solving process.
- Be kind, patient, and respectful to people as you engage with them, knowing that their reactions might be affected by their lived experience, or past hurts.
- Make sure safe spaces are created for people to engage in gatherings. Safe spaces should offer protection from physical harm and verbal harassment (i.e., a gathering where different opinions are welcomed and not met with retribution).

Redefining poverty through the lens of human dignity and justice is not merely a philosophical exercise but a call to action. We are asked to shed our preconceived notions, challenge systemic inequalities, and actively work toward creating a world where every human being can live with dignity, opportunity, and hope. By embracing this paradigm shift, we can collectively forge a path toward a more just, compassionate, and equitable society—one where the inherent worth of every individual is celebrated and protected.

Redefining Poverty

In the end, our commitment to upholding human dignity in the face of poverty is not just about alleviating material deprivation. It is about recognizing the inextricable link between poverty and the erosion of human rights, dignity, and potential. It is about acknowledging the resilience, strength, and inherent value of our neighbors who are affected by poverty and empowering them to reclaim their agency and shape their own destinies. When we redefine poverty through the lens of human dignity and justice, we can ignite a transformative movement that transcends mere charity and instead cultivates a world where every human being can thrive, flourish, and live with the dignity they deserve.

Imagine that you are holding a one-of-a-kind kaleidoscope in your hands. When you bring the kaleidoscope up to your eye, you are suddenly able to view your entire community, including the least visible members in it, as it really, truly is. A light turn of the hand yields another close-up view of a different corner of the place you call home. Give your scope a tiny twist and the doors to the homes of people who seldom cross your mind swing wide open. Who are these people? Why are they hurting? Who are they missing? Why is it so hard for them to get hired, or get to work, or keep a job? Why are their children struggling, and what are their struggles? Does your kaleidoscope reveal any evidence of a community that cares?

Seeing your community through new eyes will involve a shift in some, if not all, of the following perspectives on the reality of poverty.

- Income and consumption levels are among the most fundamental indicators of poverty. However, income alone does not paint a complete picture, as it fails to capture the multidimensional nature of poverty. Factors such as access to public services, social protection programs, and informal support networks significantly influence an individual's or household's ability to meet their needs, even with limited income.
- Adequate nutrition is a fundamental human right and a crucial component of overall well-being. Yet, millions of people worldwide experience food insecurity, which can

have severe consequences, particularly for children and vulnerable populations. Malnutrition leads to stunted growth, developmental delays, and increased susceptibility to diseases, perpetuating a cycle of poverty and poor health outcomes.

- Access to safe drinking water and adequate sanitation facilities is crucial for maintaining good health and preventing the spread of waterborne diseases. However, many communities, particularly in rural and marginalized areas, lack access to these basic amenities, thereby hindering educational and economic opportunities.
- Lack of access to basic healthcare (preventive care, diagnosis, and treatment) exacerbates existing health issues and leads to chronic conditions that further perpetuate the cycle of poverty. Indicators such as the availability of skilled healthcare professionals, access to essential medicines, and the utilization of maternal and child health services provide insights into the healthcare disparities faced by impoverished communities.
- Education is a powerful tool for breaking the intergenerational cycle of poverty. However, many children and youth from low-income households face significant barriers to accessing quality education, including the inability to afford school fees, lack of transportation, and the need to contribute to household income through labor.
- Inadequate housing and poor living conditions have far-reaching consequences on physical and mental health, as well as overall well-being. Indicators such as the proportion of the population living in slums or informal settlements, overcrowding, and access to

basic amenities like electricity and clean cooking fuels provide insights into the living conditions of the poor and their associated risks.

- Decent work and sustainable livelihoods are crucial for lifting individuals and households out of poverty. Nonetheless, many individuals living in poverty face significant barriers to accessing stable and well-paying employment opportunities, which often leads to informal or precarious work.
- The poor are disproportionately affected by environmental hazards and the impacts of climate change, as they frequently lack the resources and infrastructure to adapt and mitigate these risks. Indicators such as exposure to natural disasters, access to early warning systems, and the availability of disaster risk reduction strategies demonstrate the vulnerability of impoverished communities and their ability to cope with environmental shocks.
- Poverty is often exacerbated by social exclusion and marginalization, where certain groups face discrimination and barriers to accessing opportunities and resources based on factors such as ethnicity, religion, disability, or socioeconomic status.
- Women and girls are disproportionately affected by poverty due to various forms of gender-based discrimination and inequality. Indicators such as the gender gap in education, employment, and political representation, as well as the prevalence of gender-based violence and harmful cultural practices highlight the intersections between gender inequality and poverty.

By delving into these key poverty indicators, we gain a nuanced understanding of the multifaceted nature of poverty and its far-reaching consequences. Each indicator serves as a lens through which we can examine the disparities and injustices experienced by people living in poverty, shedding light on the intersecting challenges they face and the urgent need for comprehensive and targeted interventions. Ultimately, when we embrace a multidimensional and evidence-based approach to understanding poverty indicators, we are positioned to develop effective strategies and policies that prioritize the well-being and empowerment of vulnerable populations, fostering an equitable and inclusive society for all.

CHAPTER 3

ENCOUNTERING CHRIST THROUGH ONE ANOTHER

It would be naive to think that the apostles of Jesus experienced one, and only one, moment of conversion; namely, when they were called by Jesus to follow him. For the apostles, another major conversion experience was the passion and death of Jesus. Just as the apostles witnessed (from a safe distance) the suffering and death of Jesus, we too are called to come face-to-face with the suffering of God's people and the reality of God's mercy and compassion. With this in mind, the third week of the Spiritual Exercises is designed to lead us to a deeper union with our Lord as we contemplate Jesus's passion and death and pray for the strength to carry out our mission to alleviate the suffering of God's people. In many ways, praying for the graces of sorrow, grief, and tears might not seem like the road to the joy of union with Christ. Still, by entering more deeply into Jesus's suffering and death, we will be able to rejoice more fully in his resurrection.

In post-pandemic New Orleans, you didn't have to look very hard to find experiences of suffering that provoked sorrow, grief, and tears. As I mentioned earlier, moving home to New Orleans toward the end of the pandemic revealed just how dire the realities were as people struggled to survive in the city. Recurring crimes in the city were carjackings and car break-ins.

I was not immune.

One of the main events organized by the Office of Black Catholic Ministries for the Archdiocese of New Orleans is the annual Martin Luther King Jr. Day of Service. Since we were just emerging from the pandemic, we decided that instead of gathering folks together we would encourage groups to organize service projects at their local parish, school, or organization. The Saturday evening before the day of service, I was in my office double-checking last-minute e-mails and communications about the events when my friend who had gotten out of surgery earlier that day called, asking if I would bring him some groceries. I left my office and made my way to the store.

When I got to a stop sign at a side street there was a car in front of me. After several seconds of idling, I gently tapped my horn. As soon as I did this, a young man got out of the passenger side of the vehicle. He was wearing a ski mask and had a gun in tow. My heart started pounding. I did not know what to do. I remember staring at my rosary that hangs from the rearview mirror. And I started to pray. As he was walking toward the driver-side door I cracked my door so the interior light could show that my hands were raised. As he got to me with the gun pointed straight at me, I said, "Look man, just take it."

I was trying to get out of the car when I glanced at him. His eyes got big. He took off running, leaped back into his vehicle and, one second later, his car was in motion. He sped off leaving me there with my hands up and confused. After calming down, the only thought that came to mind was, *Is he one of my kids* (meaning, a former youth group member or student)? As I would later share the story, this possibility kept coming up as the most logical explanation for the would-be carjacker's change of heart. Although I may never know who that young man was, the incident compelled me to throw myself fully into an initiative to prevent people from choosing that path. Though the initiative was known by a thoroughly contemporary moniker—Squash the Beef—it was a modern and totally relatable name for the type of community involvement modeled by none other than Jesus.

Around the time of this incident, I received a call from a friend and collaborator, Willie Muhammad, a local Muslim imam and student minister with whom I had worked on various ecumenical community advocacy projects over the years. He said he was relaunching The Peacekeepers Initiative to advertise a conflict resolution hotline for community members to call. In response, we would arrive seeking to ease tensions between individuals or groups before it turned into violence. We invested, often with our own money, in billboards and yard signs inviting people to "squash the beef"—our slogan for resolving conflict before it erupted into violence. Minister Willie and I trained members of various faith-based groups in conflict resolution and hosted presentations from community leaders to educate them about the realities of why these incidents occur in our community. We also spent many afternoons canvassing the community with fliers and yard signs promoting the conflict resolution hotline.

The work of the Peacekeepers was a direct response to what I experienced during the aborted carjacking. In these efforts, I had a good role model. Perhaps Jesus felt something similar about his mission to what I was feeling about ours. I felt it was my responsibility, as a person of faith, to address the issue of how violence harms our communities, which was the same motivation for everyone who worked with the Peacekeepers. At the forefront, no matter what our religion might be, we made sure we understood we were doing God's work.

My experience with The Peacekeepers Initiative reminded me of the Stations of the Cross during Lent. In New Orleans, as is true everywhere, there are people at every turn of the head who are shouldering crushing burdens. The crosses they carry are heavy. Some people are forgotten. Many have been exploited. Far too many are bruised and abused, broken and battered, and weary with the weight of the crosses they carry.

Just as Jesus was condemned to death in the first station, we fight the criminal justice system that has resulted in New Orleans being dubbed "the mass incarceration capital of the world." As I have witnessed many of my fellow social activists fight for a just society, it reminds me of Jesus carrying his cross in the second station. When I have witnessed my youth struggling because of the poor education system in Louisiana, I think about Jesus falling the first time in the third station. When I have been present with priests and deacons who have sat with mothers who have lost children to violence or incarceration, I am reminded of when Jesus met his mother in the fourth station. When I witness our faith-based groups standing alongside those on the margins, it reminds me of Simon of Cyrene helping Jesus to carry his cross in the fifth station. When I have seen community organizations and political leaders rallying around a specific cause for the marginalized, I am reminded of Veronica wiping the face of Jesus in the sixth station. When I witness the harsh sentencing that our black and brown youth receive, I am reminded of Jesus falling the second time in the seventh station. When I have participated in bringing our elders to get their errands run, or to just keep them company, I envision Jesus meeting with the women of Jerusalem in the eight station. When I have witnessed homeless encampments broken up to prepare for a large tourist event, I am envisioning Jesus falling a third time as in the ninth station. When I see news stories degrading and demonizing our black and brown youth based on unjust stereotypes, I think of Jesus being stripped of his garments in the tenth station. When I have attended city meetings where the elected officials have chosen unjust policies that hurt the marginalized, I am reminded of Jesus being nailed to the cross in the eleventh station. When I have participated in community healing events after a murder, or various other tragedies, I think of Jesus dying on the cross in the twelfth station. When I have seen the heartache of fellow community activists whose lives are negatively impacted because of their dedication to creating a just society, I think of Jesus being taken down from the cross in the thirteenth station. Finally, when I suffer through a funeral service of a young person in my community, especially a death caused by violence, I think about Jesus being laid in his tomb as in the fourteenth station.

We must continue to pray with our feet and be motivated by our faith to help the marginalized carry their burden. This is why we pray with our feet. This is where we pray with our feet. This is when we look to Jesus to know what we must do. Remember, it is not about us, but about what God does through us to bring forth his kingdom here on earth.

At the heart of Kwanzaa is the principle of Ujima, which states that we are called to make my community's problems, my problems. It would be easy to hide within our church walls and pretend that the problems outside do not exist, or do not affect us, but Jesus challenges us to live and think differently. If the margins of society are calling out to us for help, then so too is God calling out from the margins.

To really live out our baptismal call, we must actually become disciples, which is to say evangelists, for Christ. We must actually *do* for others. We must go to those in need and then use our gifts and talents to help these people. This path is challenging and countercultural in a capitalistic society, but since when were we called to do the popular thing? The easy thing? No, we were called to do the right thing. The just thing. We are called to have empathy with suffering, be it mental, physical, emotional, or spiritual. And this empathy is supposed to move us to action. As Pope Francis wrote in *Fratelli Tutti*, "The existence of each and every individual is deeply tied to that of others: life is not simply time that passes; life is a time for interactions."[17] This is our chance to live a meaningful life. To make a difference.

Reclaiming Dignity and Empathy

The language we use to discuss issues of injustice, healing, and reconciliation is powerfully impactful. Understanding the meanings and implications of key terms is crucial for effectively navigating complex and sensitive topics. To that end, I offer the following baseline definitions:

> We must continue to pray with our feet and be motivated by our faith to help the marginalized carry their burden. This is why we pray with our feet. This is where we pray with our feet. This is when we look to Jesus to know what we must do.

- **Dignity:** often reduced to a mere buzzword, the essence of dignity lies in recognizing the inherent worth and respect owed to every human being, regardless of their circumstances. Dignity is a fundamental principle that acknowledges the equal and inalienable rights we all possess by virtue of our shared humanity. Dignity is not a privilege to be earned or granted; it is an intrinsic quality that exists within us whether or not we are treated respectfully. To be human is to embody dignity. To uphold dignity is to behave kindly, respectfully, always conscious of the other person's unique value and worth. Upholding dignity means rejecting the dehumanization and marginalization of any individual or group, and actively working toward creating a society where everyone's inherent dignity is honored and protected.

- **Empathy:** more than just a fleeting emotional response, empathy is a profound capacity to step into the lived experiences of other people. Another way of putting it is that empathy involves transcending the boundaries of our own perspectives. What empathy is *not* is a fleeting moment of sympathy or emotional resonance. Empathy requires an openness not just to *listen* to people, but to *hear* them. To be empathetic involves suspending our own biases and preconceptions about people whose realities differ from our own. Empathy is a critical component in the healing process, as it allows us to create spaces of understanding, validation, and solidarity, laying the groundwork for meaningful dialogue and collective growth.
- **Reconciliation:** a process that demands courage, vulnerability, and a willingness to confront painful truths about ourselves and our culpability; reconciliation can be a complex, arduous journey. On the other hand, when people are in alignment regarding the issues and end goals, reconciliation can be surprisingly direct. Either way, being a co-creator in the reconciling process is incredibly rewarding; restoring broken relationships, rebuilding trust, and addressing the root causes of conflict and injustice is hard work that "pays" well. Reconciliation requires a commitment to open and honest dialogue, where all parties are given the opportunity to share their experiences, grievances, and perspectives without judgment. It also necessitates a willingness to take responsibility for past harms, to acknowledge wrongdoings, and to actively work toward making amends. Ultimately, reconciliation is not

merely about forgiveness; neither is it about forgetting. Reconciliation is about creating a shared understanding, fostering empathy and respect, and collaborating to make a better way.

- **Restoration:** as we embark on a transformative journey toward wholeness, restoration is where the scars of injustice become catalysts for health, progress, and optimism. Restoration requires a holistic approach to engage with the multifaceted impacts of injustice, including psychological, emotional, and spiritual dimensions. It involves nurturing a sense of belonging, self-worth, and empowerment within marginalized communities. True restoration is a collaborative process that amplifies the voices of our neighbors who have been silenced, and creates spaces for their narratives to be heard, validated, and integrated into the fabric of society.
- **Healing Language:** a powerful tool that can either perpetuate cycles of oppression or ignite sparks of understanding and connection, healing language guides us toward a more equitable and humane society. Healing language rejects dehumanizing rhetoric, harmful stereotypes, and the reinforcement of oppressive narratives. Instead, healing language seeks to uplift, validate, and empower people who have been marginalized. It is a language that fosters dialogue, promotes understanding, and challenges us to confront our own biases and assumptions. Healing language is not about political correctness or censorship; it is about cultivating a culture of compassion, where our words have the power to bridge divides.

These terms—dignity, empathy, reconciliation, restoration, and healing language—serve as guideposts on our collective journey. It is up to us to be respectful of the power that language holds, and be aware of our responsibility to wield this power mindfully.

Justice Redefined: A Holistic Perspective

As Dr. King famously wrote in his "Letter from a Birmingham Jail," dated April 16, 1963, "Injustice anywhere is a threat to justice everywhere."[18] The concept of justice has been a cornerstone of human civilization, yet the traditional notion of justice, often rooted in retribution and punishment, falls short of addressing the complex and multifaceted nature of harm, oppression, and systemic inequities. Justice, in its holistic form, is a dynamic and all-encompassing framework that transcends the narrow confines of legal systems and punitive measures. It is a state of being where every individual is treated with dignity, respect, and equity. Holistic justice restores balance, heals wounds, and transforms narratives of power and privilege, enabling individuals and communities to thrive in an environment of mutual understanding, empathy, and solidarity. A short definition of terms will put us all on the same wavelength of understanding holistic justice. The fundamental components of justice are as follows:

- **Personal Justice:** this aspect encompasses the individual's pursuit of self-awareness, healing, and personal growth. It involves confronting our own biases, acknowledging privileges, and developing empathy and compassion toward oneself and other people who may live differently than we do.

- **Interpersonal Justice:** this dimension focuses on the restoration of relationships, the fostering of forgiveness, and the cultivation of mutual understanding and respect among individuals and communities.
- **Systemic Justice:** this component addresses the deeply entrenched societal structures, policies, and practices that perpetuate marginalization, discrimination, and oppression. It calls for the demolishing of unjust systems and the creation of equitable and inclusive frameworks that uplift all members of society.
- **Environmental Justice:** this facet recognizes the inextricable link between human well-being and the health of our planet. It advocates for the protection of natural resources, sustainable practices, and the preservation of our shared ecosystem for current and future generations.
- **Restorative Justice:** this approach emphasizes accountability, healing, and the restoration of dignity for all parties involved in conflict or harm. It seeks to address the root causes of injustice and promote transformative solutions that foster reconciliation and lasting societal change.

Unfortunately, the traditional Western approach to justice has long been rooted in retributive models, focusing primarily on punishment for the maintenance of societal order. This narrow perspective has frequently failed to address the underlying causes of injustice; worse, it is guilty of perpetuating cycles of harm and marginalization. Embracing a holistic understanding of justice is essential for creating a more equitable, inclusive, safe, and sustainable world. It recognizes that true justice cannot be achieved through fragmented or siloed approaches, but rather requires a comprehensive and intersectional perspective that addresses the interconnected nature of personal, interpersonal, systemic, and environmental challenges.

By redefining justice within this holistic framework, we can reshape narratives of power and privilege, undo oppressive structures, and foster transformative healing at both individual and collective levels. A paradigm shift like this empowers communities to reclaim their agency, amplify marginalized voices, and collectively work toward a future where every human being can thrive in an atmosphere of mutual understanding, respect, and dignity. This is exactly what happened when people got together to do something about desperate acts, like carjacking, and their efforts to "squash the beef"—a community solved a problem when given the proper resources and hope. That is the power of communities of faith connecting to do the work of praying with their feet. The hope we demonstrate through our actions can inspire a community to change.

Injustice, oppression, and inequality are often rooted in systems and structures that perpetuate marginalization and silence the voices of the people who are impacted. In confronting these challenges, an evidence-based approach is crucial to amplifying the experiences and realities of affected communities, fostering empathy, and driving meaningful systemic transformation. Authentic advocacy and sustainable social change require a deep understanding of the lived experiences and testimonies of marginalized individuals and groups, coupled with robust data and research that quantify the extent and impact of injustice.

Personal testimonies humanize abstract concepts and statistics. The visceral and tangible quality of these narratives challenge indifference and apathy, compelling individuals and societies to confront injustice. It is important to hear from the people themselves, especially those on the margins. We should not make decisions without those affected by the decisions being at the table. Just as we see nonprofits and fundraising efforts allowing those they serve to tell their stories, we, as people of faith, should empower all in our community to be allowed to tell their story so those who are in power can understand the true nature of what needs to be done to address the issues at hand.

It is important to hear from the people themselves, especially those on the margins. We should not make decisions without those affected by the decisions being at the table.

Furthermore, the act of sharing testimonies can be a powerful form of resistance and reclamation of agency for people who have been silenced or marginalized, allowing them to reclaim their narratives, assert their humanity, and demand recognition for their struggles and resilience. At the same time, it is essential to recognize that personal testimonies and empirical data are not mutually exclusive but rather complementary components of an effective evidence-based advocacy approach. By combining the raw emotional power of personal narratives with the rigor and objectivity of quantitative data and research, a comprehensive and compelling case for change can be presented.

Praying with Our Feet: The Catholic Social Teaching of Call to Family, Community, and Participation

The Catholic social teaching of call to family, community, and participation summons us to build a communal spirit and promote the well-being of all by supporting families and their communities. As followers of Jesus, we are called to participate in a community of faith—the Church. For Catholics, faith is not a "me-and-God" experience, but rather a "we-and-God" experience; following Jesus and recognizing God's presence in daily living is not an individual experience but a communal relation.

God's very essence is relationality. One of the most central beliefs of Christianity is our belief in a triune God—Father, Son, and Holy Spirit—a community of Persons whose love is so strong and intimate that God is One. As human beings made in the image and likeness of our triune God, we are called to build and nourish relationships and form what I like to call "beloved communities."

Across movements and generations, the concept of a "beloved community" has been invoked as a guiding vision, inspiring individuals and collectives to work toward a society rooted in justice, solidarity, and reconciliation. Yet, the depth and breadth of what it entails often remains elusive, leaving us to ponder the true essence of this aspiration. As a reminder, the beloved community is a community in which everyone is cared for, absent of hate, poverty, and hunger. Dr. King, fueled by his faith, believed that such a community was, in fact, possible. Dr. King always acknowledged that realizing this vision would involve systems of education, law, healthcare, and infrastructure, among other factors—no one area, much less an individual, could create it in isolation. It is a community effort. One example of such a community is the early Christian groups who connected in love and faith under the threat of persecution.

> For Catholics, faith is not a "me-and-God" experience, but rather a "we-and-God" experience; following Jesus and recognizing God's presence in daily living is not an individual experience but a communal relation.

At its core, the beloved community demands a radical shift in perspective, one that recognizes the fundamental interconnectedness of all beings and embraces the inherent dignity and worth of every individual. It necessitates a profound commitment to challenging systems of oppression and entrenched biases, and actively cultivating spaces where diversity is celebrated, compassion is nurtured, and the voices of the marginalized are amplified and honored. An example is the Beloved Community Center in Greensboro, North Carolina, which emerged from the legacy of the 1960 Greensboro sit-ins and serves as a hub for community organizing, social justice education, and intergenerational healing. Yet another inspiring initiative is the Beloved Community Village in Denver, Colorado, which provides transitional housing, support services, and a nurturing environment for people experiencing homelessness, centering their lived experiences and promoting community self-governance.

Building a beloved community is not a destination but a continual journey of growth, healing, and collective transformation. It requires each of us to embark on a personal journey of unlearning and relearning, to cultivate empathy, humility, and a deep commitment to justice. And it calls upon us to engage in courageous conversations, to confront our biases, and to actively work toward challenging systems of oppression that continue to perpetuate harm and marginalization.

To take meaningful action toward fostering a beloved community, we can:

- Engage in ongoing self-education and critical analysis of power dynamics, privilege, and systemic oppression;
- Seek out and amplify voices from marginalized communities, and actively listen to their lived experiences, perspectives, and wisdom;
- Participate in restorative justice initiatives, community dialogues, and collaborative problem-solving processes that center the voices and experiences of people most impacted by injustice;
- Support grassroots organizations, community-led initiatives, and movements that embody the principles of a beloved community and work toward transformative social change;
- Cultivate spaces for healing, cultural expression, and intergenerational dialogue, where diverse identities and experiences are honored and celebrated;
- Advocate for policies, practices, and resource allocation that prioritize equity, justice, and the redistribution of power and resources to historically marginalized communities; and
- Embrace a lifelong commitment to personal growth, accountability, and the ongoing work of undoing internalized biases and oppressive mindsets.

By embracing the profound depth and breadth of building a beloved community, we can reimagine a world where justice, solidarity, and reconciliation are not mere aspirations but lived realities woven into the fabric of our societies. It is a journey that demands our unwavering commitment, our collective courage, and our willingness to continually evolve and grow toward a more just, equitable, and authentically beloved world.

Defining Beloved Community: Essential Elements and Principles

To understand the depth and breadth of what it means to build a beloved community, we must first delve into the foundational elements and principles that shape its essence. The following concepts are not mere abstract ideals but essential guideposts that illuminate the path forward.

- **Justice:** more than just a legal concept, justice is the cornerstone of a beloved community.
- **Solidarity:** actions and feelings of unity that manifest in a deep understanding of each other's struggles, a willingness to share in the collective burden, and a commitment to standing together in the face of injustice.
- **Reconciliation:** transcending mere forgiveness, reconciliation challenges us to confront painful histories, acknowledge harm, and engage in the difficult work of healing, restoration, and transformation.

Throughout history, communities have been fractured by forces of oppression, discrimination, and marginalization, leaving deep wounds that fester and undermine the pursuit of genuine unity and belonging. However, by embracing a transformative approach rooted in principles of justice, reconciliation, and collective healing, we can chart a path toward realizing the dream of a beloved community.

As we navigate the complex tapestry of diverse societies, the fabric of our communities is threatened with a myriad of divisions breaking along lines of race, ethnicity, religion, socioeconomic status, gender, sexuality, ability, and other intersecting identities. They are fueled by systemic oppression, historical trauma, and ongoing cycles of marginalization and exclusion. The negative outcomes are far-reaching and devastating—they erode trust and social cohesion, perpetuate cycles of violence and conflict, and deprive individuals and communities of the dignity and sense of belonging they deserve. When left unaddressed, these divisions undermine the very foundations of a just and equitable society, leaving behind a trail of broken relationships, unhealed trauma, and unfulfilled potential.

To overcome such divisions and create a beloved community, we must embark on a journey of intentional and transformative work to initiate a radical shift in our understanding of community-building, one that moves beyond traditional models of assimilation and conformity toward a more holistic and inclusive paradigm. The beloved community approach is grounded in the following principles:

- **Embracing Diversity as Strength:** rather than viewing diversity as a threat, we must celebrate the richness of human experiences and identities. By creating spaces where diverse voices are amplified and honored, we can tap into the collective wisdom and creativity residing within our communities.

- **Amplifying Marginalized Voices:** all too often, community-building efforts have perpetuated the marginalization of certain groups, ignoring their unique perspectives and needs. The beloved community approach centers the lived experiences of people who have been historically oppressed by ensuring that their narratives and aspirations are at the forefront of our collective efforts.
- **Restorative Justice and Healing:** genuine reconciliation and unity cannot be achieved without addressing the deep-rooted wounds of historical trauma and systemic injustice. The beloved community approach prioritizes restorative justice practices, truth-telling, and collective healing processes, recognizing that accountability, repair, and transformation are intertwined.
- **Intersectional Solidarity:** the pursuit of a beloved community requires an intersectional lens that acknowledges the interconnected nature of oppression and the importance of building coalitions across diverse identities and experiences. By fostering intersectional solidarity, we can amplify our collective power and work toward reconfiguring interconnected systems of oppression.
- **Empowerment and Collective Action:** building a beloved community is an active and ongoing process of empowerment and collective action. It requires equipping individuals and communities with the

> tools, resources, and support necessary to reclaim their agency, challenge oppressive structures, and co-create alternative systems rooted in justice and equity.

The pursuit of a beloved community has been a long, arduous, yet profoundly inspiring journey woven through the fabric of human history. We must never forget the milestones, pivotal moments, and visionary leaders who have shaped the ongoing struggle for justice, solidarity, and reconciliation, illuminating progress made and challenges yet to overcome. From the legacies of slavery, colonialism, and institutional racism to the widening economic inequalities, climate crisis, and conflicts and human rights violations around the world, the journey toward beloved communities within a just and equitable society remains an unfinished task. Yet, the historical timeline also serves as a testament to the resilience, courage, and unwavering commitment of countless people and earnest movements who refused to accept the status quo and fought relentlessly for a world where every human being is valued, respected, and empowered to thrive. As we confront the challenges of our time, we must draw inspiration from this rich tapestry of resistance, recognizing that the realization of a beloved community is not a destination but an ongoing journey requiring collective action, unwavering hope, and a profound commitment to progress.

Let us be guided by the wisdom of our community members who have walked this path before us, while remaining open to continuous learning, adaptation, and the integration of diverse perspectives and experiences. For it is through this unwavering commitment to evidence, collaboration, and a shared vision of justice where we can effectively manifest the beloved community—a world where every individual is celebrated, supported, and empowered to thrive to their fullest potential. Here are some ways to practice beloved community principles:

- Looking at different cultural and socioeconomic segments in our society, how are various family realities supported to thrive? A first step to take is to learn about the different types of families in your community.
- What policies need to be changed so that the most vulnerable families have the same opportunities to thrive as community members who are more affluent?
- Consider ways of addressing the lack of opportunities for the youth to have safe places to play and socialize. Partner with and give your support to nonprofits and organizations that are doing this work.
- The reality of families broken up by the criminal justice system is inescapable. Research organizations that address this issue and shed light in your own community on how you can support their work.
- What are some ways to extend our church family beyond our parish or organization walls? How can we better connect with organizations and groups to enlarge participation in various events?
- Promote and participate in events from different cultural or socioeconomic groups as you are welcomed and/or invited to do so.
- What are some work/life balance issues that need to be addressed to allow families to be present with each other? What events and gatherings can you facilitate to help families spend more quality time together?

When Dr. King discussed the beloved community, he was referring to a society governed by love. In 1957, in the pages of *Ebony* magazine, he explained further, writing, "Love is creative and redemptive. Love builds up and unites; hate tears down and destroys. . . . Physical force can repress, restrain, coerce, destroy, but it cannot create and organize anything permanent; only love can do that. Yes, love—which means understanding, creative, redemptive goodwill, even for one's enemies—is the solution to the race problem."[19]

This philosophy could solve a host of problems we face even still today and no doubt will face in the future. Dr. King was asking us—reminding us—to love our neighbors as we love ourselves, just as Jesus commands us to do. Dr. King was asking us to look beyond those things that divide us, in the hope of trying to understand each other. This is how the beloved community comes into existence.

Praying with Our Feet: The Catholic Social Teaching of Rights and Responsibilities

The Catholic social teaching of rights and responsibilities reminds us that human dignity must be protected and healthy communities can be built only if human rights are protected, and we each take responsibility for making this a reality. We all have the duty and responsibility to protect the rights of one another, of families, and of our democratic society.

In Baptism, each of us gains a share in Jesus's priestly, prophetic, and kingly role. With these roles come specific responsibilities about how to care for the needs of our neighbors. In the prophetic ministry, our call is to speak on God's behalf in advocacy of people whose rights are being violated and trampled. Too often, we tend to view injustice as an abstract concept, as if it is detached from our lived realities; this makes it easy to dismiss injustice as someone else's burden to bear, which means, of course, that it's someone else's problem to fix. We often fail to recognize the pervasive and insidious nature of systemic oppression woven into the fabric of our institutions, policies, and societal norms. Coupled with a reluctance to confront uncomfortable truths, this lack of awareness perpetuates a cycle of inaction and complacency.

Another common misconception is the belief that being "not racist" or "not discriminating" is enough to combat injustice. However, this passive approach ignores the reality that injustice thrives on indifference and inaction. The gospel calls us to be "anti-racist." This requires a willingness to get engaged in courageous conversations, to listen deeply to the lived experiences of people impacted by injustice, and to confront our own biases, privileges, and complicity in oppressive systems.

Consider the ongoing struggle for racial justice in the United States. Despite the progress made through the civil rights movement and federal legislation, systemic racism persists, manifesting in disparities in education, housing, employment, healthcare, and the criminal justice system. True commitment to racial justice requires acknowledging these disparities but also engaging in difficult dialogues about the legacy of slavery, the impact of discriminatory policies, and the ways in which white privilege and internalized biases perpetuate these inequities.

Some people may argue that confronting injustice is too daunting a task, that the problems are too entrenched to tackle, and some may claim that addressing injustice will inevitably create division or backlash. However, these objections fail to recognize the moral imperative of standing up against oppression and the long-term societal costs of allowing injustice to fester. But there is another side to these fear-inducing considerations, and that other side is where the rewards await. Courageous conversations, when approached with empathy and a genuine desire for understanding, foster unity and collective healing, which are no small things.

In the face of systemic inequalities and oppressive structures, a provocative question arises: Are you ready to speak out against injustice? This question cuts to the core of our moral and ethical obligations as members of a shared humanity.

Throughout history, oppressive systems have thrived on the silence and complicity of people who witness injustice. But in moments of profound courage, individuals and movements rise up to challenge the status quo, refusing to remain silent in the face of oppression. The power of speaking out has proven to be a catalyst for social transformation.

Speaking out against injustice extends far beyond any single issue or community. It speaks to the fundamental values of human dignity, equality, and justice that should underpin our societies. When we remain silent, we allow injustice to fester and solidify, emboldening people who perpetuate harm and oppression. Confronting the painful realities of systemic inequalities is a moral imperative, a call to action demanding our collective voice and unwavering commitment to creating a more equitable and just world.

Here are a few ways to practice rights and responsibilities in everyday living:

- Look at where there is inequality in your community, and see what is being done, and needs to be done, to address it.

Are you ready to speak out against injustice? This question cuts to the core of our moral and ethical obligations as members of a shared humanity.

- Ask yourself: Do I respect the economic, social, political, and cultural rights of other community members? Where do I need to do a self-examination to understand these concepts?
- Ask yourself: Do I live in material comfort while the rights of my neighbors are unfulfilled? What can I do to help correct this imbalance? Advocate for our community members who are vulnerable by urging people in positions of power and influence to create policies and laws that support the rights of our most vulnerable brothers and sisters.
- Educate your own family and friends about the needs in your community. Create opportunities to address inequities.

As people of faith, it is our duty to look out for the needs of those most vulnerable in society. The reality of capitalism and competition divides us, but Christ calls us to live in a love that unites us.

A Prophetic Voice: Speaking Out with Courage and Conviction

To confront injustice and achieve transformative change, we must embrace a prophetic voice, one that speaks truth to power, challenges oppressive systems, and amplifies the voices of the marginalized. This prophetic voice is grounded in a deep sense of moral courage, a willingness to confront uncomfortable truths, and an unwavering commitment to justice and equity. Speaking out with a prophetic voice involves more than mere words; it requires a holistic approach that combines education, advocacy, and direct action. As we interrogate our own biases, privileges, and complicity in perpetuating oppressive structures, the prophetic voice calls us to engage in difficult conversations, challenge harmful narratives, and dismantle the systems that uphold injustice.

The prophetic voice is not limited to our neighbors directly impacted by injustice; it is a clarion call for all who believe in the inherent dignity and worth of every human being, a rallying cry for allies and accomplices to stand in solidarity with marginalized communities while using their platforms and privileges to amplify long-silenced voices. The power of a prophetic voice has been demonstrated time and again throughout history, serving as a beacon of hope and a catalyst for transformative change. The civil rights movement, led by visionaries like Dr. King and many other activists, harnessed the power of prophetic speech to challenge the brutality of racial segregation and discrimination. Their voices reverberated across the nation, igniting a movement that toppled legal barriers and shifted cultural narratives.

More recently, the Black Lives Matter movement has embodied a prophetic voice, unapologetically confronting systemic racism, police brutality, and the dehumanization of Black lives. Through powerful rhetoric, direct action, and a refusal to remain silent, this movement has inspired a global reckoning with racial injustice and a renewed commitment to undoing oppressive structures.

Silence Is Not an Option

While the call to speak out against injustice is a moral imperative, it is not without challenges and potential objections. Some may argue that speaking out is futile, pointing to the entrenched nature of oppressive systems and the resistance to change; others still may claim that speaking out is divisive or polarizing, potentially exacerbating tensions and conflicts. However, history has shown that even the most formidable barriers can be overcome through sustained, collective action and a refusal to remain silent. True progress requires confronting uncomfortable truths and challenging the status quo. Injustice thrives in silence and complacency, and a prophetic voice is necessary to disrupt oppressive narratives and systems.

There may also be concerns about personal risks or consequences associated with speaking out, such as backlash, retaliation, or even physical harm. These concerns are valid and underscore the need for collective action, allyship, and the creation of supportive networks and safe spaces for community advocates who raise their voices against injustice.

To confront injustice and create lasting change, each of us must embrace our prophetic voice and speak out with courage and conviction. This involves taking concrete steps to educate ourselves, amplify marginalized voices, and engage in sustained activism and advocacy.

First, it is crucial to commit to ongoing learning and self-reflection. Seek out resources, literature, and perspectives that challenge your assumptions and expand your understanding of systemic oppression. Engage in difficult conversations, listen to the lived experiences of marginalized communities, and confront your own biases and complicity in perpetuating injustice.

Next, use your platform and privilege to amplify the voices of people who have been silenced or marginalized. Uplift their narratives, share their stories, and create spaces where their experiences and perspectives can be heard and valued. Advocate for their inclusion and representation in decision-making processes and positions of power.

Additionally, engage in direct action and sustained activism. Join or support movements and organizations that are actively working to dismantle oppressive systems and promote equity and justice. Participate in protests, rallies, and community organizing efforts that challenge injustice and demand systemic change.

Finally, cultivate resilience and build supportive networks. Speaking out against injustice can be emotionally and psychologically taxing, and it is essential to prioritize self-care and collective healing. Surround yourself with a community of allies and accomplices who can offer support, encouragement, and a shared commitment to the struggle for justice.

In the face of injustice, silence is complicity. The time has come to embrace our prophetic voices and speak out with awareness and unwavering conviction.

In the ongoing struggle for social justice and equity, awareness plays a pivotal role. Understanding systemic barriers, oppressive structures, and deeply rooted inequities is the first step toward meaningful change. Awareness alone, however, is not enough. True transformation requires a transition from passive recognition to active engagement—a mobilization that translates knowledge into tangible actions aimed at destroying oppressive systems and promoting justice for all.

Despite increasing awareness of social injustices, our world remains mired in a state of inaction and complacency. We bear witness to the marginalization of communities, the perpetuation of systemic discrimination, and the erosion of civil liberties, yet our collective response often falls short. This inertia stems from various sources: fear, apathy, a sense of powerlessness, or the belief that change is too daunting a task. Whatever the underlying reasons, the consequences of inaction are grave: if oppressive structures remain unchallenged, inequities and the suffering of marginalized groups will continue unabated.

The urgency for change cannot be overstated. Each day that passes without meaningful action is a day in which injustice prevails, human rights are violated, and the principles of equity and dignity are compromised. The impact of inaction reverberates across generations, perpetuating cycles of oppression and denying human beings the opportunity to live with dignity, freedom, and equal access to opportunities. Inaction is not a neutral stance; it is an implicit endorsement of the status quo, a tacit acceptance of injustice.

The solution lies in a collective mobilization—a call to action that transcends boundaries and unites us in the pursuit of justice and equity. This mobilization must be multifaceted, encompassing a range of strategic actions tailored to address the specific challenges at hand. It may involve grassroots organizing, advocacy efforts, legal challenges, policy reforms, educational initiatives, and the amplification of marginalized voices. The key is to channel our awareness into purposeful, coordinated efforts that dismantle oppressive systems and disrupt the status quo.

Defining the Prophetic Tradition: A Call to Action

Imagine a voice that resonates with moral clarity, cutting through the noise of complacency and challenging the systems that perpetuate oppression. This is the prophetic voice—a clarion call reverberating through time, summoning us to confront injustice and embrace the responsibility to create a more equitable world. But what is the true essence of a prophetic voice?

The prophetic voice is not merely a metaphor; it is a powerful call to action that echoes through the annals of history. From the ancient Hebrew prophets who confronted injustice and spoke truth to power, to modern-day social justice warriors, the prophetic voice has been a catalyst for transformation. It is a voice that refuses to be silenced, a voice that amplifies the cries of the marginalized and challenges the status quo. At the heart of the prophetic voice lies a deep sense of moral courage—a willingness to confront uncomfortable truths and to speak out against injustice, even in the face of adversity. As it transcends boundaries and resonates across cultures, the prophetic voice inspires individuals to embrace their inherent worth and to fight for a world in which justice and equity reign supreme.

The prophetic tradition within Catholic social teaching and Ignatian spirituality is a sacred quilt, woven from the threads of faith, justice, and compassion. It is a clear and impactful message to actively engage in the pursuit of human dignity, to defend the rights of the oppressed, and to challenge the systems that perpetuate inequality and marginalization. In the teachings of the Catholic Church, we find a resounding call for social justice, rooted in the belief that every human being is created in the image of God and therefore deserving of respect, dignity, and equal opportunities. From the encyclicals of popes to the voices of inspirational figures like Dorothy Day and St. Óscar Romero, the prophetic tradition echoes through the ages, reminding us of our moral obligation to stand with the marginalized and to work toward a more just and equitable world.

In the teachings of the Catholic Church, we find a resounding call for social justice, rooted in the belief that every human being is created in the image of God and therefore deserving of respect, dignity, and equal opportunities.

Ignatian spirituality, too, is imbued with a prophetic spirit that compels us to seek God in all things, and to embrace a life of service and social responsibility. St. Ignatius of Loyola's teachings emphasize the importance of discernment, reflection, and a commitment to finding meaning and purpose in the pursuit of justice. Through the practice of the Spiritual Exercises, individuals are invited to embark on a transformative journey, awakening to the realities of injustice and embracing their role as agents of change. As we embark on this journey of exploring the prophetic tradition, we are invited to become more than mere observers; we are called to embrace our own prophetic voices and to actively participate in the pursuit of justice.

The Promise of a Just and Equitable Society

While the path toward systemic transformation is undoubtedly challenging, the rewards of our collective efforts are immeasurable. A society free from the shackles of systemic injustice is a society where every individual has the opportunity to thrive, where human potential is unleashed, and where the principles of equity, dignity, and justice are not mere aspirations but lived realities. By challenging the barriers that have limited opportunities and stifled progress for generations, we open the doors to a world of boundless possibilities. We create a society where every child, regardless of their circumstances, can pursue their own personal destiny, where innovation and creativity flourish, and where the tapestry of our diversity is celebrated and embraced.

While prophetic voices have inspired transformative change, their journeys have often been marked by immense challenges, persecution, and opposition from entrenched powers. From the martyrdom of early Christian prophets to the imprisonment of Nelson Mandela, these obstacles have tested the resolve of people who dare to envision a better world. Disputes and schisms within movements have sometimes threatened to undermine their prophetic vision, as differing interpretations and priorities emerge. The civil rights movement, for instance, witnessed tensions between advocates of nonviolent resistance and those calling for more radical action. So too has the environmental movement grappled with conflicting narratives surrounding sustainable development and preservation. Yet, these pivotal moments have also served a purpose, which was to refine and strengthen the prophetic vision, inspiring new generations of activists and thinkers to carry the torch of justice and equality forward, adapting and evolving in the face of ever-changing circumstances and emerging challenges.

In a world grappling with persistent inequalities, systemic oppression, and environmental degradation, the need for a compelling vision of justice rooted in prophetic values has never been more pressing. Prophetic advocacy has always been at the forefront of challenging entrenched systems of oppression and injustice. Whether confronting racial discrimination, economic exploitation, or gender-based violence, prophetic voices have courageously exposed the structures and ideologies that perpetuate inequality and marginalization. By confronting power, privilege, and vested interests—while promoting transformative solutions at the root of injustice—we can dismantle the barriers that prevent marginalized communities from realizing their full potential and thriving in a just and equitable society. And in embracing prophetic values and strategies, we can envision a world where justice is not merely an abstract concept but a lived reality.

The journey toward collective healing and reconciliation is one that requires us to celebrate our diversity while simultaneously recognizing the threads that bind us together. It is a delicate balance, one that demands openness, empathy, and willingness to embrace the beauty and richness that emanates from our differences. When we extend our hands in unity, embracing the tapestry of our shared humanity, we unlock the potential for profound transformation—a transformation that heals wounds, bridges divides, and paves the way for a more just, inclusive, and harmonious world.

CHAPTER 4

EMPOWERING ALL COMMUNITY MEMBERS TO SHINE THEIR LIGHT

The fourth week of St. Ignatius's Spiritual Exercises invites us to contemplate the resurrection of Jesus Christ and our total, deep, and generous response of love to God's gifts. In many ways, the goal of the fourth week is to embrace what should be the permanent disposition of Christians: one of joy and hope, accompanied by a refusal to submit to despair amid suffering. An important contemplation made during the fourth week is the resurrection of Jesus Christ; another significant contemplation is the Pentecostal coming of the Holy Spirit. Although the apostles experienced conversion as a result of the passion, death, and resurrection of Jesus, they were slow to understand and embrace the meaning of the Resurrection. This, of course, sets the stage for the ultimate conversion that occurs at Pentecost.

The graces of Pentecost compel us to go forth into the world as missionary disciples of Jesus Christ, armed with the confident hope that St. Paul spoke of when he asserted that nothing—*nothing*—can separate us from the love of God in Christ Jesus (Romans 8:39). It is this fortitude that also enabled St. Paul to insist: "We are afflicted in every way, but not crushed; perplexed, but not driven to despair; persecuted, but not forsaken; struck down, but not destroyed; always carrying in the body the death of Jesus, so that the life of Jesus may also be made visible in our bodies" (2 Corinthians 4:8-10).

It is easy to tell ourselves *That was then; this is now*, and just keep moving. But the Holy Spirit is very much on the move—especially today. One of the greatest blessings in my ministerial career has been doing presentations on various topics at conferences around the country. Even though I have done hundreds of presentations over several decades, each invitation puts me in awe that God would use me in such a way. While such occasions are enriching experiences, they are not void of challenges. My personal struggle is that I do not travel well, due to allergies and motion sickness which make it a physical sacrifice to get to and from such events.

One of my favorite conferences to attend is the Los Angeles Religious Education Congress where I am able to reconnect with folks from different ministry backgrounds and speak with some of my ministry heroes, people like Fr. Gregory Boyle, SJ, and Sr. Helen Prejean, among others. I was very ill when I attended in 2022, and I spent any non-workshop time in my room taking all kinds of cold and flu medication to knock it out of my system. Of course, the meds made it difficult to fall asleep and left me feeling groggy. After my final workshop, it was time to limp home to New Orleans. I could not wait to get on the plane so I could sleep.

As the boarding process was nearing completion, I realized that the middle seat next to me was open. I thanked God because I wanted to stretch out. Evidently I spoke too soon. The last person to board the flight was a burly White gentleman who looked like a stereotypical biker. He saw me sitting in the window seat, smiled as he pointed to the middle seat, and said, "I guess I'm here." Both of our large selves then moved and shifted so we could fit into the row. As the plane took off, I put my head back in search of sleep. Before long, however, the gentleman turned my way and said, "It's never easy being two big guys in the same row." I gave a polite laugh and prayed silently that God allow me to get some sleep. However, since he proceeded to make small talk, I told myself silently, "Okay, Lord. I guess this is what we're going to do today." When my seat neighbor asked if I was from California, I said no, I was in town for a ministry conference. He paused and said, "Really? I'm mad at God." I knew immediately that sleep was not what God had in mind for me.

I met his gaze. He was crying. I asked, "Brother, what's going on?" He proceeded to tell me that he lost his wife and son to a car accident a year ago and he was struggling. I did my best to focus and be present for him. When he realized that I was genuinely concerned, he shared that he was in Orange County for his first ever date since the loss of his wife and he was feeling guilty. I offered a perspective that his wife, but also God, wants him to be happy, and encouraged him not to feel sad about trying to search for companionship and happiness. The conversation continued for the rest of the flight, and after we landed, he walked me to my gate. Our time together concluded with us exchanging numbers, and me offering a prayer for him and his situation. To this day, we keep each other updated on life.

I would never have thought that this encounter would be the reason God had me travel to California. I do not recall any of my other encounters during that trip, but this one stays with me. I was given an opportunity to experience God's love by sharing his love with one of his struggling children. No matter the circumstances, Christians are called to spread joy, which is a fruit of the Spirit that intrigues and draws people in. Although I was caught off guard by the gentleman's statement about being angry with God, the experience of connecting with him on the flight, despite my grogginess, was an opening to witness God's love for him in that moment.

Sharing Peace in a Struggling World

Right now is our moment to share peace in a struggling world. We know that Christ's resurrection means that death does not have the last word. So too must we believe that no matter what the world may be experiencing, our hope in the Resurrection compels us to spread joy everywhere we go in pursuit of a just society.

At times, however, the pursuit of justice and mercy can be tainted by ulterior motives or misguided assumptions. Some people might be in pursuit of justice and mercy as a means of gaining power, influence, or personal recognition; others might approach the work of establishing justice and mercy with a sense of moral superiority, looking down upon people they deem oppressors or wrongdoers, and failing to recognize their own biases and shortcomings. A common misconception is that the pursuit of justice and mercy is solely a matter of external action, which is to say protesting against, advocating for, or helping to enact policies and laws.

> **No matter the circumstances, Christians are called to spread joy, which is a fruit of the Spirit that intrigues and draws people in.**

While these external efforts are undoubtedly important, they can be rendered ineffective or even counterproductive if they are not accompanied by an inward journey of self-awareness and personal transformation. To embody the spirit of justice and mercy, our pursuit must be grounded in a deep sense of humility, compassion, and a genuine desire for collective liberation. This approach calls for us to engage in a continuous process of self-examination, challenging our own biases, privileges, and assumptions that might perpetuate harm or hinder our ability to empathize with those on the margins.

One of the ways to be effective in performing this introspection is by praying the Examen. Through this prayer experience, St. Ignatius invites us to find God in all things. We are reminded to be acutely aware of the movements of the Holy Spirit in every aspect of our lives as it calls us to deeply analyze the ordinary to encounter the divine. The power of the Examen is that it invites us to encounter God, share our appreciation for the daily gifts we are given, and atone for any mistakes that were made during the day. The beauty of this prayer is that it can be molded to meet many of the needs of our times (anti-racism, the global pandemic, ecology, and so on). The Jesuit website (see: https://www.jesuits.org/spirituality/the-ignatian-examen/) features various adaptions of this powerful prayer which calls us to put our inner reflections into action.

Consider the example of the civil rights movement in the United States, where leaders like Dr. King and Bayard Rustin emphasized the importance of nonviolent resistance and moral suasion. Their approach was rooted in an unwavering belief in the inherent dignity of all human beings, regardless of race or background. By appealing to the conscience of their oppressors and embracing a philosophy of unconditional love, which moved them to action, they were able to catalyze transformative change and challenge deeply entrenched systems of oppression. Another example can be found in the work of organizations like the Truth and Reconciliation Commission in South Africa, which sought to address the legacy of apartheid by creating spaces for victims and perpetrators to share their stories, acknowledge past wrongs, and allow healing and reconciliation to unfold. This approach recognized that true justice cannot be achieved through retribution alone, but rather through a process of restorative justice that fosters empathy, understanding, and a shared commitment to building a more just and inclusive society.

Some might argue that embracing humility and compassion in the pursuit of justice and mercy could be perceived as weakness or a lack of resolve. However, this perspective fails to recognize that true strength lies in the ability to confront injustice with unwavering moral courage while simultaneously extending empathy and understanding toward those who have perpetrated harm.

Ignatian Spirituality, Contemplation, and Action

At first glance, the word *contemplation* might evoke images of serene monasteries or solitary meditation retreats; notwithstanding, contemplation holds a deeper, more potent meaning in the context of social justice. A contemplative practice invites us to step back from the frenetic pace of activism and immerse ourselves in profound reflection, allowing insights to emerge from the depths of our consciousness. The concept of mindfulness has also gained widespread recognition in recent years; its true power lies in its ability to cultivate a state of heightened awareness and presence that leads to action. By embracing mindfulness, we learn to observe our thoughts, emotions, and biases without judgment, enabling us to engage with societal issues from a place of clarity and compassion.

Ignatian spirituality provides us with the elements needed to connect contemplation and action:

- **Discernment** is the art of separating truth from illusion, of cutting through the noise and distractions that cloud our perception. In the realm of social justice, discernment empowers us to see beyond surface-level manifestations of oppression and identify the underlying systemic forces at play, guiding our actions toward lasting transformation.
- **Wisdom** is not merely the accumulation of knowledge but the ability to apply that knowledge with clarity, compassion, and a deep understanding of interconnectedness. In our pursuit of social change, wisdom enables us to navigate complex situations, make ethical

decisions, and cultivate a holistic approach that considers the intricate web of societal systems and their impact on marginalized communities.
- **Insight** is the profound understanding that arises from contemplation, mindfulness, and discernment. It is the "aha" moment that illuminates the root causes of oppression and reveals the path forward toward systemic transformation. Insight is the catalyst that propels us from reactive responses to proactive, transformative action.

In the Ignatian tradition, contemplation is so much more than mere luxury, or a retreat from the challenges of social justice work. Contemplation is a powerful tool that shapes our understanding, sharpens our discernment, and ultimately guides us toward effective and lasting change. Contemplation invites us to do three things: embrace stillness amid the chaos, quiet the incessant chatter of the mind, and create space within which profound insights can emerge. It is in moments of silence and reflection when we gain a deeper understanding of the systemic forces and ideologies that perpetuate oppression.

Contemplation in action can be defined as a process of intentional, spiritually grounded reflection and discernment, which in turn fuels purposeful, socially transformative engagement. As a holistic approach harmonizing inner work and outer action, contemplation recognizes that sustainable social change demands both personal growth and strategic activism. At its core, contemplation in action involves cultivating a heightened awareness of oneself, one's community, and the broader societal landscape. Through practices like meditation, prayer, or mindful contemplation, people develop a deeper understanding of their values, beliefs, and purpose. This self-knowledge serves as a catalyst for aligning personal aspirations with a commitment to social justice and positive change.

Moreover, contemplation in action recognizes that individual reflections can have a ripple effect, contributing to collective societal shifts. When people engage in contemplative practices and prayerful discernment, they become engines for change within their immediate circles of influence. Transformed perspectives inspire people, igniting a chain reaction that reshapes cultural narratives, challenges systemic injustices, and ultimately paves the way for more equitable and inclusive societies.

Becoming Agents of Change

The call to be an agent of change goes beyond charity and short-term relief efforts, summoning us instead to an essential understanding of the systemic roots of oppression, and an impassioned commitment to addressing the underlying causes of injustice. Since true spiritual growth demands that we not only tend to our purgation but also to the purgation of the world around us, becoming an agent of change requires us to confront our own biases and complacencies, to challenge the status quo, and to stand firm in the face of opposition from people who benefit from the perpetuation of injustice. It is a journey that will test our resolve, our empathy, and our willingness to step outside the confines of our comfort zones. Yet, it is also a path that holds the promise of profound personal and societal transformation. By embracing the inextricable link between spirituality and social justice, we open ourselves to a deeper understanding of our interconnectedness with all of humanity. We become agents of change, channels through which the divine love and compassion that animates our faith can flow into the world, healing wounds and restoring hope.

Consider the powerful examples set by figures like Archbishop Óscar Romero, who paid the ultimate price for his unwavering commitment to the poor and oppressed in El Salvador. Or Dorothy Day, whose life was a testament to the seamless integration of her Catholic faith and her activism for social justice. The life of the late Bishop Harold Perry, SVD, the first African American bishop of modern times, witnesses to the commitment to social justice in the face of oppression and resistance. Or the countless unsung heroes, from grassroots organizers to courageous whistleblowers, who have risked everything to shine a light on injustice and advocate for the vulnerable.

These people understood that the Christian faith is not a private or passive pursuit but a sacred call to action, and their lives serve as a reminder that our spiritual growth is inextricably linked to our commitment to justice, compassion, and the upliftment of the downtrodden. They show us that, if we wish to embody the principles of Catholic social teaching and Ignatian spirituality, we must be willing to venture into unfamiliar territory, to listen to voices that have been silenced, and to confront the uncomfortable truths that lie at the heart of systemic injustice.

The Call to Ecological Conversion, or Baptized When the Levees Broke

August 2005 changed my life forever. Hurricane Katrina robbed me of nineteen family members and friends, including the love of my life. I lost my residence, my community. I evacuated to various states until the waters flooding New Orleans were drained. Upon return, Fr. Mike, my pastor and mentor, asked that I guard our church from vandals.

During the day I would work to clean it out in preparation for the contractor. At night I would sleep in the balcony so that I could thwart an attempted break-in. The next few years were like a bad dream. Not only was the corruption of local, state, and federal governments revealed, but we also learned some tough lessons about our fragile relationship with Mother Nature. Fighting to bring back my community and addressing the injustices inflicted upon the poor of the region revealed that this could happen again. Hurricane season in this region of Louisiana has everyone living in cautious fear because we are keenly aware that we are not in control.

As we go about our daily lives, immersed in the busyness of modern society, it's easy to overlook the impact our actions have on the delicate ecosystems that sustain life on earth. Yet, with each passing day, the consequences of our collective disregard for the environment become more severe, more undeniable. What will happen if we continue to turn a blind eye to the cries of our fragile planet, its forests dwindling, its oceans choking, its climate in turmoil?

The urgency of ecological conversion is not merely a scientific or political issue, it is a moral and spiritual imperative that demands our attention and action. As stewards of this remarkable planet, we are called to a profound transformation, a shift in our consciousness and behavior that recognizes the intrinsic value of all life as well as our sacred responsibility to protect and nurture the natural world.

The interconnectedness of all things is a fundamental truth that lies at the heart of Ignatian spirituality. Just as our personal journeys are woven into the tapestry of the divine, so too are our actions intertwined with the well-being of the earth. We cannot separate our spiritual growth from our relationship with the environment, for in being conscientious caretakers of the earth, we honor the Creator and embrace the call to live in harmony with all creation.

The consequences of our individual and collective actions are laid bare before us. Deforestation, pollution, and the relentless exploitation of natural resources have pushed our planet to the brink. Climate change, once a distant concern, now manifests in increasingly severe weather patterns, rising sea levels, and the displacement of vulnerable communities. Biodiversity, the rich tapestry of life that sustains our ecosystems, is under threat as habitats are destroyed and species face extinction. These changes are not abstract concepts—they are tangible realities structuring the lives of every human being on earth. Poverty, hunger, and political conflict resulting from ecological collapses and climate conflict are inevitable. And the poor and marginalized—in other words, those who are least culpable in causing these real-life crises—are the very people who will inevitably be trapped bearing the brunt of the disastrous consequences of our fast-changing climate.

> The interconnectedness of all things is a fundamental truth that lies at the heart of Ignatian spirituality. Just as our personal journeys are woven into the tapestry of the divine, so too are our actions intertwined with the well-being of the earth.

In the face of such daunting challenges, it can be tempting for all of us who care to succumb to despair, or to seek solace in half-measures and false solutions. Some of us may rest our hopes on technological advances that will provide a panacea, while others may cling to the notion that economic growth and unfettered consumption are necessary for human progress. These misconceptions often end up becoming ineffective approaches that fail to address the root causes of our ecological crisis. Worse, they perpetuate the very behaviors that have brought us to this precipice.

Healing Practices: Cultivating Compassion and Justice

In the pursuit of social justice and the transformation of oppressive systems, it is essential to cultivate compassion and nurture a sense of shared humanity. Let's explore some practical strategies and rituals that promote healing, foster empathy, and nurture a culture of solidarity and care.

- **Circle Process:** the circle process is a powerful tool for creating a safe, inclusive space where dialogue, reflection, and healing can occur. When forming a physical circle, participants are reminded of their interconnectedness and the equality that is inherent in the shared human experience. This sacred space is where people can safely share their stories, vulnerabilities, and perspectives without judgment or interruption. The circle process fosters listening, empathy, and a sense of community, laying the foundation for collaborative problem-solving and collective healing.

- **Storytelling and Testimony:** amplifying the voices and lived experiences of people who live in marginalized communities is a crucial component of cultivating compassion and driving systemic change. By sharing personal narratives and testimonies, people who have endured injustice and oppression reclaim their agency and assert their humanity. These stories have the power to evoke empathy, challenge indifference, and inspire people to deal with oppressive structures. Storytelling and testimony can take various forms, including oral histories, written accounts, art, music, or multimedia presentations. All are viable methods for ensuring that the narratives of people we are inviting into the fold of wholeness and high regard are preserved, shared, and woven into the collective consciousness.
- **Rituals of Remembrance:** throughout history, communities have found solace and strength in rituals that honor people who have suffered injustice and oppression. These rituals serve as powerful reminders of the resilience and sacrifices of previous generations, who helped instill in us a sense of reverence and motivation for continuing our struggle for justice. Rituals may include vigils, memorial services, or ceremonies

that incorporate cultural or spiritual elements, such as prayer, song, dance, or other culturally relevant spiritual practices. By engaging in these practices, everyone can connect with one another through our shared histories. We can heal from collective trauma. And we can renew our commitment to addressing ongoing injustices.

- **Contemplative Practices:** cultivating compassion and justice begins with self-awareness and inner transformation. Contemplative practices such as mindfulness meditation, reflective journaling, and guided visualizations instigate the exploration of biases, assumptions, and inherited but outdated narratives. These practices foster self-compassion, emotional regulation, and the ability to hold space for discomfort and difficult emotions. By developing these skills, we become better equipped to confront injustice with clarity, empathy, and resilience, and we are more able to recognize and feel our interconnectedness.
- **Creative Expression:** art, music, dance, prayer, both private and communal, and other creative modalities offer powerful avenues for processing trauma, expressing difficult emotions, and promoting healing. Through these expressive outlets, we give voice to our experiences, explore complex narratives, and find solace, satisfaction, and fulfillment in the act of creation. Creative expression also serves as a catalyst for community building. Participatory art projects, community murals, and collaborative dramatic and musical performances bring people together, amplify marginalized voices, and inspire collective action for social change.

- **Ancestral Wisdom and Indigenous Practices:** Indigenous communities around the world have developed rich traditions and practices rooted in their deep connections to the land, their ancestors, and their spiritual beliefs. These practices offer invaluable insights into the cultivation of compassion, healing, and the restoration of balance and harmony. By learning from Indigenous wisdom keepers and elders, we can all gain a deeper appreciation for the interconnectedness of life, the importance of reciprocity and respect for the natural world, and the power of collective healing. Practices such as smudging ceremonies, talking circles, or the use of traditional medicines and plants can provide pathways for reconnecting with ancestral knowledge and fostering a more holistic approach to justice and well-being.

Healing practices that cultivate empathy, foster shared understanding, and promote collective healing serve as powerful tools for amplifying marginalized voices. By integrating these rituals and actions into our personal and communal lives, we can create a foundation for meaningful and sustainable change.

Praying with Our Feet: The Catholic Social Teaching of Care for God's Creation

The Catholic social teaching of care for God's creation reminds us that we are called to care for all that God has made. The Church further reminds us that our proclamation of the gospel must "help believers become aware that the commitment to the environmental question is an integral part of the Christian life."[20] To care for God's creation is to be pro-life (since our planet sustains human life).

Pope Francis, who took his name from the Church's patron saint of ecology and animals, St. Francis of Assisi, writes passionately about our call to care for God's creation in his encyclical, *Laudato Si'*:

> Along with the importance of little everyday gestures, social love moves us to devise larger strategies to halt environmental degradation and to encourage a "culture of care" which permeates all of society. When we feel that God is calling us to intervene with others in these social dynamics, we should realize that this too is part of our spirituality, which is an exercise of charity and, as such, matures and sanctifies us.[21]

Knowing Pope Francis's abiding respect for all of creation, it is not surprising that he is a member of the Society of Jesus. As a Jesuit, Pope Francis would know a great deal about Ignatian spirituality, the central tenet of which is to see God in all things. Transformative change begins within each of us when we cultivate a heightened awareness of our impact on the environment and a subsequent willingness to make adjustments to our lifestyles and consumption patterns. In our communities, we must advocate for sustainable practices, support eco-friendly initiatives, and hold our leaders accountable for their actions.

True ecological conversion demands a systemic shift in our societal values and priorities. We must challenge the prevailing paradigm of exploitative and extractive practices, questioning the very foundations of an economic system that prioritizes short-term gains over long-term sustainability. We must embrace a new vision of development that respects the limits of our planet's resources and, at the same time, upholds the dignity of all life.

The path of ecological conversion is one of spiritual growth and practical action, which calls us to cultivate a deep reverence for the natural world, marvel at the intricate beauty of creation, and recognize our role as co-creators and caretakers of this precious gift. Such reverence for God's creation manifests in tangible actions like reducing our carbon footprint, supporting sustainable agriculture, and protecting biodiversity. Ecological conversion also motivates us to advocate for policies that prioritize environmental justice, ensuring that the burdens of ecological degradation are not disproportionately borne by the most vulnerable. Moreover, it inspires us to collaborate with different groups, transcending boundaries and fostering a global movement of ecological solidarity, for just as the earth's ecosystems are interconnected, so too must our efforts be united in a shared vision of a thriving, sustainable planet.

Back home in New Orleans, many studies were conducted on how Mississippi River diversions, sinking land masses, changing climate, and other factors impacted the devastating effects of Hurricane Katrina. These studies, and various local conversations, resulted in new perspectives for the citizens of Southeast Louisiana living near water. One of the new innovations that came about is the Mirabeau Water Garden, which will create ways for water to run through neighborhoods to reduce flood risks while also creating opportunities for present and future generations to appreciate and care for the local environment.

Undoubtedly, the call for ecological conversion will face skepticism and resistance. Some may argue that environmental concerns must take a backseat to economic priorities, or that the sacrifices required are too great. Some may question the efficacy of individual actions or the feasibility of large-scale systemic change. Yet, these objections fail to acknowledge the grave consequences of inaction and the mounting costs of ecological degradation. Worse, they ignore the moral imperative to protect the earth for future generations. But climate change skeptics underestimate the power of collective action and the transformative potential of a shared commitment to a sustainable future.

The steps along the path of ecological conversion are indeed numerous and unpredictable, yet what they share in common are intention and purpose. It is important that we move forward while examining the root causes of environmental issues that various communities face. We must educate ourselves and our communities, raising awareness of the urgency of ecological issues and the interconnectedness of all life. We must embrace sustainable practices in our daily lives, reducing our carbon footprint and supporting eco-friendly initiatives. And we must also engage in advocacy and activism, calling upon our leaders and institutions to prioritize environmental protection and sustainable development, which may involve supporting policies that promote renewable energy, protect natural habitats, and address the disproportionate impact of environmental degradation on marginalized communities.

Furthermore, we must foster a sense of global solidarity, recognizing that the health of our planet is a shared responsibility and that our efforts must transcend national boundaries. This may involve participating in international forums, supporting global initiatives, and collaborating with organizations and communities across the world. Ultimately, the path of ecological conversion is a journey of transformation—a transformation of our individual consciousness, our societal values, and our relationship with the natural world. It is a journey that demands courage, perseverance, and a deep commitment to preserving the beauty and diversity of life on our fragile planet.

As we navigate this path, we must remain steadfast in our conviction, drawing strength from our faith and the wisdom of Ignatian spirituality. For in embracing ecological conversion, we honor the divine spark within all creation, and we fulfill our sacred duty as stewards of the remarkable gift we call earth. Our quest requires us to be familiar with several critical principles:

- **Ecological Conversion as a Holistic Metamorphosis:** imagine a caterpillar, bound by its earthly existence, yet harboring the potential for a breathtaking metamorphosis. Much like this transformative process, ecological conversion represents a holistic shift in our consciousness, one in which we transcend the confines of our current paradigms to embrace a profound reverence for the intricate web of life that sustains our planet.
- **Sustainability as a Delicate Balance:** sustainability is not merely a buzzword or a fad or fleeting trend. Sustainability is a fundamental principle that recognizes the delicate equilibrium between human activity and the earth's finite resources. To embrace sustainability is to acknowledge our role as stewards of this fragile planet, striving to meet our present needs without compromising the viability of future generations to meet their own.
- **Spiritual Ecology as a Sacred Interconnectedness:** at the heart of ecological conversion lies the concept of spiritual ecology, which is the profound understanding that our spiritual journey is inextricably intertwined with

the well-being of the natural world. Just as we nurture our souls through prayer and contemplation, we must also nurture the earth, recognizing the sacred interconnectedness that binds all life in a harmonious tapestry.

- **Environmental Justice as Upholding Dignity for All:** environmental degradation often disproportionately impacts marginalized communities, exacerbating existing inequalities and thereby perpetuating cycles of poverty and vulnerability. Environmental justice seeks to address these disparities, ensuring that all people, regardless of race, socioeconomic status, or geographic location, have equal access to a clean and healthy environment.
- **Global Solidarity as United in Purpose:** the challenges we face in protecting our planet transcend national boundaries and cultural divides. Global solidarity represents a shared commitment to preserving the earth's ecosystems, fostering international cooperation, and recognizing that our collective actions have far-reaching consequences for all of humanity.

In his encyclical *Laudato Si´* Pope Francis says, "Environmental problems cannot be separated from . . . how individuals relate to themselves."[22] He is reminding us that we are all interconnected in the shared space we call earth, and it is our responsibility to make sure all are able to survive and thrive, no matter their location or socioeconomic status.

Environmental Stewardship

Stewardship refers to the caretaking of something valuable that has been entrusted to us. Stewards do not own or possess. We hold in stewardship something that has great value. Environmental stewardship is not merely a lofty ideal but a tangible, actionable pursuit. It is a call to embrace our interconnectedness with the natural world, to honor the delicate balance that sustains life, and to leave a legacy of resilience and regeneration for generations to come.

As environmental stewards, we must remain open to learning from diverse perspectives, engaging with local communities, and fostering interdisciplinary collaborations. By bridging the divide between tradition and innovation, between Indigenous knowledge systems and modern scientific inquiry, we can unlock the transformative potential of eco-friendly practices and inspire a global movement toward a sustainable, resilient, and harmonious coexistence with the natural world.

If left unchecked, the repercussions of climate change will be catastrophic. Worldwide, rising sea levels could displace hundreds of millions of people living in coastal regions, while prolonged droughts and shifting weather patterns, resulting in stronger storms, could severely disrupt agricultural systems, leading to food shortages and widespread famine. Moreover, the loss of biodiversity will irreparably damage the delicate ecosystems that sustain life on our planet, setting off a chain reaction of ecological collapse.

As we stand at the precipice of a new era, the earth's delicate equilibrium hangs in the balance, teetering under the weight of human activity. The climate crisis, once a distant whisper, has evolved into a blaring roar that can no longer be ignored.

The scale and scope of this crisis are staggering, transcending geographical boundaries and threatening the very foundation of life as we know it.

Ecological Ethics: Nurturing a Values-Based Approach

Imagine a world where every thread of existence is intricately woven into a vast tapestry, a masterpiece of interconnected life-forms, each strand representing a unique species or ecosystem. Now, envision the gradual fraying of this tapestry as human actions unravel the design, leaving behind a tattered canvas of environmental degradation. This haunting metaphor underscores the urgency of embracing ecological ethics, a value-based approach that guides our decisions and actions to nurture, rather than ravage, the intricate web of life that sustains us.

At its core, ecological ethics is a philosophical framework that recognizes the inherent value of the natural world and the moral imperative to protect and preserve it. It underscores the interdependence between humans and the environment, emphasizing our responsibility to act as stewards of the earth's resources and ecosystems. An ecologically based ethical paradigm transcends utilitarianism by acknowledging that the environment holds intrinsic worth beyond its utility to humankind.

The foundation of ecological ethics rests on three fundamental pillars:

- **Respect:** recognizing the inherent worth of all life forms and their right to exist and thrive, free from unnecessary harm or exploitation.

- **Responsibility:** embracing our role as caretakers of the natural world, making conscious choices that minimize our environmental impact and promote sustainable practices.
- **Reverence:** cultivating appreciation and awe for the beauty, mystery, complexity, and resilience of the natural world, fostering a sense of humility and interconnectedness.

Ecological ethics extends far beyond theoretical constructs; it is a living, breathing ethos that permeates every aspect of our lives and decision-making processes. From individual choices to corporate policies, from urban planning to global governance, this values-based approach serves as a compass for shaping a sustainable future. In our daily lives, ecological ethics encourages us to adopt eco-friendly practices, including reducing energy consumption, minimizing waste, and supporting sustainable agriculture such as choosing organic fertilizer over its chemically destructive counterparts. It prompts us to make mindful choices as consumers, prioritizing where to shop when we buy products and services that align with environmental stewardship principles. Something as simple as carrying a refillable water bottle rather than using disposable water bottles can make an impact over time. On a broader scale, ecological ethics informs policy decisions, urging governments and industries to prioritize environmental protection, implement sustainable practices, and invest in renewable energy sources. It challenges us to rethink our economic models, moving away from the extractive and exploitative paradigms that have fueled environmental degradation and toward a more regenerative and circular approach.

Embracing ecological ethics has the potential to ignite a ripple effect that radiates outward, influencing communities, nations, and ultimately, global consciousness. As more individuals and organizations adopt this values-based approach, a collective shift toward environmental stewardship will emerge, fostering a renewed sense of responsibility and urgency in addressing pressing ecological challenges. Educational institutions can integrate these principles into their curricula, empowering future generations with the knowledge and values necessary to create a more sustainable world. Faith-based organizations may choose to leverage their moral authority to promote environmental stewardship as a sacred duty, and corporations can align their business practices with ecological ethics, demonstrating that profitability and environmental responsibility are not mutually exclusive.

> We must do this work together, not in silos. Jesus himself modeled this work ethic. Yes, he had the power to solve the issues of his time, but he chose to encounter and accompany those on the margins and helped them realize their own power in addressing the ills of their era.

In the face of escalating environmental crises, embracing ecological ethics is a moral imperative, a call to action, a summons to reshape our relationship with the natural world and reclaim our role as custodians of this precious planet. As we weave this values-based approach into the fabric of our societies, we can mend the tattered tapestry of existence, restoring the harmony and balance that once defined our interconnectedness with the environment.

The path toward ecological renewal is a journey we must undertake with unwavering commitment and a shared sense of responsibility. Each step we take, every decision we make, carries the weight of generations to come, echoing across the vast expanse of time and shaping the legacy we leave behind. To be effective advocates in ecological renewal, along with other social justice issues, we must work with intersectionality, in conjunction with other groups and communities. We must do this work together, not in silos. Jesus himself modeled this work ethic. Yes, he had the power to solve the issues of his time, but he chose to encounter and accompany those on the margins and helped them realize their own power in addressing the ills of their era. So too are we called to engage with others, and their unique challenges, to solve our problems together. This is the power of encountering God in the margins.

Raising Awareness

One of the most powerful actions we can take is to raise awareness and inspire people to join a sustainability movement. Study, read, share knowledge, lead by example, and engage in environmental advocacy efforts. Participate in community forums, educational initiatives, or social media campaigns to promote eco-friendly practices and encourage collective action toward a greener future. And take a very close look at how you live your own life. When it comes to ecology, just like everything else, the more we learn, the more we realize that there is more to be learned. And the more we do, the more we understand that there is more to be done.

By embracing these eco-actions and integrating them into our daily lives, we can collectively contribute to the preservation of our planet's natural resources and the well-being of future generations. It is important to remember that every small action counts, but by working together, we can create a ripple effect of positive change toward a more sustainable world. Here are a few ways to practice care for God's creation in everyday living:

> To pray with our feet is to see God in all things.

- **Intentionally connect with** creation by being outside and witnessing God's majesty in the world he created in various environments.
- **Study** ways through which you and your loved ones can reduce waste within your own home; then, learn about the products and services used in your community, share this knowledge with others, and together brainstorm how you can help at the local level. The local library is a great resource for all of these efforts, including offering space where meetings can be held.
- **Learn** about how climate change affects our neighbors in poverty. Educate people and partner with organizations addressing this issue.
- **Create** venues and events where people can learn more about the environment and how ecological ethics ties into our faith lives.
- **Speak to** your elected officials and advocate for laws and policies that create legal protections for the environment.
- **Educate** young people on how to care for the environment so that they can continue this practice as they grow into adulthood.

As we conclude our journey together, I would ask you to reflect on the following question: Are we truly living in accordance with the principles of justice and mercy to create a just society and lives of holiness, despite the challenges of the modern world? This question strikes at the very core of our existence as individuals and as a society because it challenges us to examine our actions, beliefs, and the systems we have constructed through the lens of equity, compassion, and human dignity. If we answer this question by living lives of holiness, the fruit of our actions will transcend boundaries and resonate across cultures, generations, and lived experiences. We must remember, just as Christ lived and died to create a more just and merciful world, we are called to have the same sense of justice and love for our fellow human beings. This is our faith lived out.

To pray with our feet is to see God in all things. Our experience of holiness expands when we seek and know the presence of Jesus, not only in the Body of Christ as it comes to us in the Eucharist, but also in the Body of Christ that is our Church, our brothers and sisters, our fellow pilgrims on planet earth. We are all "made in the image and likeness of God," and thus we all need to look at where we can do more to help to build the kingdom of God here on earth.[23]

Let us continue to seek out authentic ways to put our faith into action. Let us see God in everything. Let us encounter God in everyone. Let us find God everywhere. Let us go, then, everywhere, but most especially to the least, the last, the lost, and the powerless living in the margins of society, as we pray with our feet.

EPILOGUE

HOLD FAST TO THE FLAME OF HOPE

And so, as we journey together toward a transformed world, let us hold fast to the flame of hope that burns within us. Let us draw inspiration from countless people like you and me living in communities similar to ours, people who have walked this path before us, leaving a trail of wisdom, courage, and unwavering faith in their wake. Let us be unafraid to imagine a world where justice, equity, and compassion reign supreme. A world in which the inherent dignity of every human being is honored. A world in which the pursuit of the common good is the driving force behind every decision. A world where we live in true solidarity with one another, united in our shared humanity and our collective commitment to creating a better future for all.

Let us be unafraid to imagine a world where justice, equity, and compassion reign supreme.

For it is in daring to imagine such a world that we ignite the spark of hope that will light our way toward its realization. And it is through our faith-inspired actions, guided by the principles of Catholic social teaching and Ignatian spirituality, that we will fan those flames into a radiant blaze, illuminating the path toward a transformed world.

As we stand at the crossroads, the narratives that sing of our shared destiny resound. Each one transcends the divisions of the past and embraces the possibilities of the future. It is that spark for justice, growing into a flame of collective action, that calls upon each of us to be agents of change, that lends our voices to the chorus of justice and the sacred responsibility of creating a world that is worthy of our highest aspirations. This is the vision that beckons us, the clarion call that resonates through the ages, inviting us to join hands and hearts in pursuit of a just society. A world where the principles of equality, liberty, and solidarity are not mere abstractions but living, breathing realities. It is a vision that demands our unwavering commitment, our collective courage, and our relentless determination to bend the arc of history toward justice.

From the ongoing legacies of slavery, colonialism, and institutional racism, to widening economic inequalities, climate crises, and ongoing conflicts and human rights violations around the world, the journey toward a just and equitable society remains an unfinished task. Yet, the historical timeline also serves as a testament to the resilience, courage, and unwavering commitment of countless people and earnest movements who refused to accept the status quo and fought relentlessly for a world where every human being is valued, respected, and empowered to thrive. As we confront the challenges of our time, we must draw inspiration from this tapestry of resistance, recognizing that the realization of a beloved community is not a destination but an ongoing journey that requires collective action, unwavering hope, and a profound commitment to progress.

Let us be guided by the wisdom of our community members who have walked this path before us, while remaining open to continuous learning, adaptation, and the integration of diverse perspectives and experiences. For it is through this unwavering commitment to evidence, collaboration, and a shared vision of justice that we can effectively manifest the beloved community. A world where every individual is celebrated, supported, and empowered to thrive in their fullest potential.

It is time that we, as a Church, pray with our feet better than we have ever done before!

AFTERWORD

CALL AND RESPONSE

With the opening announcement of *Praying with Our Feet*, Dr. Ansel Augustine situates himself in a unique place in the sacred circle that symbolizes and illustrates our faith: He is the guide of the crossroads, challenging the reader to understand where we are and why we stand where we stand, and then to decide how we must move together to the place where we can best live out our responsibilities as children of the Covenant. Dr. Augustine starts with a quotation from "What We Have Seen and Heard," the Black Catholic bishops' 1984 pastoral letter: "Let us who are the children of pain now be a bridge of reconciliation. Let us who are the offspring of violence become the channels of compassion. Let us, the sons and daughters of bondage, be the bringers of peace."[24]

With "What We Have Seen and Heard," the Black Catholic bishops shift the focus that is found in the Great Covenant, first in the Book of Exodus and then in the Gospel according to Matthew. The bishops take on the role of the "others" who are to be the subjects of the work of the chosen ones. In Exodus, God says, "You shall not wrong or oppress a resident alien, for you were aliens in the land of Egypt. You shall not abuse any widow or orphan. If you do abuse them, when they cry out to me, I will surely heed their cry" (Exodus 22:21–22). The bishops—and Ansel Augustine—identify themselves as the descendants of those who once were deemed the alien, the other, the outcast, the downtrodden. And these who once were marginalized and talked about (or ignored) are now proclaiming what must be done in order for the Covenant to be honored.

The voiceless speak.

Ansel Augustine is clear in accepting this role. Throughout this guidebook, he assumes the role of teacher, leader, guide, and companion to those who wish to follow the great commandment of Jesus the Christ: "'You shall love the Lord your God with all your heart, and with all your soul, and with all your mind.' This is the greatest and first commandment. And a second is like it: 'You shall love your neighbor as yourself.' On these two commandments hang all the law and the prophets" (Matthew 22:37–40).

Our author encourages the readers to discern who they are and who their neighbor must be—even if such a discovery means overthrowing overwhelming cultural challenges that stand in the way to true discernment and acceptance. And this call to conversion in *Praying with Our Feet* is spoken with great authority, but with absolutely no sense of hierarchical privilege. Augustine places himself in the center of the circle, pointing the way to acts of justice. By encouraging the reader to employ the Spiritual Exercises of St. Ignatius of Loyola, our guide calls us to free our imaginations from transactional prayer. We are shown how to enter into the story that presents itself to us: "See the world through the eyes of people who are different from you. Understand that your perception and experience of life is not the only reality" (see page 63). We don't recite familiar prayers for the *other*—we open ourselves to allow the *other* to dwell with us in our minds and hearts and spirit.

Dr. Augustine illustrates every lesson with stories. What else do we have, when we are honest with ourselves, but our stories? We are reminded, chapter by chapter, that we must accept the stories of those we wish to walk with, no matter where their journey commenced, because when we accept the truth of their lives, our lives are filled with grace. With his articulation of the elements of Catholic social teaching, his outline of the five notions of justice, and the connection of the Stations of the Cross to his own life and the lives of those who cry out for justice and healing, Ansel Augustine provides compelling, powerful, transformational strategies as to how this guidebook can bring grace to those who choose to follow the call of Christ.

Finally, it is nothing less than blessings poured down, running over (Luke 6:38) that we must notice the way our author lifts up in gratitude those he mentions as mentors of great power: the late Fr. Michael Jacques, SSE, and the late Bishop Fernand J. Cheri III, OFM. It has been a gift for me to see personally through the years their influence in helping Ansel Augustine persist on, growing in fullness and grace. The stories he shares of how he has manifested those gifts of guidance, instruction, and support wherever he has journeyed inspire all of us to persist too. He shows us that when we pray with our feet we are never alone, for we have the power of the Holy Spirit helping us prevail against obstacles, fears, and doubts. And when we arrive, we will find that Jesus is already there.

Ansel Augustine defines himself as a true "doctor of ministry," knowing that service for the kingdom, giving without counting the cost, finding God in all things, is the call that impels him—and us—on our journey. And we go, with Ansel in our minds and hearts, praying with our feet to heal the wounded. To become those who "Raise up the foundations of many generations; you shall be called the repairer of the breach, the restorer of streets to live in" (Isaiah 58:12).

Thank you, Ansel Augustine. Thank you.

—Joseph A. Brown, SJ, PhD
Professor, School of Africana
and Multicultural Studies
Southern Illinois University

POSTSCRIPT

GOD'S DREAM COME TRUE

Standing requires feet. Jesus never took the right stand on issues. He just chose to stand in the right place. In his Spiritual Exercises, St. Ignatius of Loyola has a meditation called the Two Standards. In it, he states simply, "See Jesus standing in the lowly place." As is outlined in this fine book, Ansel Augustine points the way for us to pray and stand at the margins. It seems to be the only way they will get systematically erased.

Love can remain sequestered in the air or the ether. Once in a while, it moves from our head to our heart. But love never becomes connective tissue, joining us in union with each other, unless it travels to our feet. Where we stand matters.

I don't go to the margins to "make a difference" because then it's about me, and it can't be. My hope is to go to the margins so that the folks there make *me* different; then it's about *us*. This is God's dream come true. See Jesus standing in the lowly place. Watch him have his heart altered by the exquisitely mutual encounter there.

Ignatius calls this *acatamiento*, "affectionate awe." It is how we cherish folks at the margins. It is how we become the notice of God in the world and tenderly cherish the demonized and easily despised. Systems change when people do. And people change when they are cherished.

The entire trajectory of God's kindness requires a humble praying with our feet and allowing us to move freely "in the lowly place."

—Greg Boyle

DEDICATION AND ACKNOWLEDGMENTS

This book is dedicated to the ancestors and elders who had the courage to make the world uncomfortable as they fought to create a just society, and to the youth and young adults doing the same today: keep shining your light in a world that needs it. This book is also dedicated to my family and friends incarcerated in Rayburn Correctional Center, the Louisiana State Penitentiary (Angola), and the Louisiana Correctional Institute for Women: thank you for continuing to be a source of faith during overwhelming trials. Also, a special dedication to the Cheri and Chase families: thank you for sharing Bishop Fernand Cheri III, OFM, and Mrs. Leah Chase (our local Disney Princess) with me, and with our world; their love for creating a just society has impacted, and continues to direct, my ministry. To my fellow culture bearers (Mardi Gras Black Masking Indians, Baby Dolls, Skeletons, Musicians, and Artists) and community activists of New Orleans: never give up the struggle to keep our home authentic and welcoming for the locals in our community. A special thank you to my brother and sister in ministry, Joe Paprocki and Maura Poston, for encouraging me to complete this project, and their assistance toward that goal. Deep thanks to Gary Jansen, who, seeing a diamond in the rough, made sure it got polished and published. I would also like to say a heartfelt thank you to Bishop Joseph Perry, Fr. Joseph Brown, and Fr. Gregory Boyle for their contributions to and support of this book. I am humbled and grateful to each of you. Finally, I want to give a special thank you to my Krewe of Pyros family for allowing me to share my passion for social advocacy, and pray with my feet, in the DMV (DC, Maryland, and Virginia) area.

ENDNOTES

1. St. Ignatius of Loyola, *The Spiritual Exercises*, 1548.
2. United State Conference of Catholic Bishops, "Two Feet of Love in Action," https://www.usccb.org/beliefs-and-teachings/what-we-believe/catholic-social-teaching/two-feet-of-love-in-action.
3. Rev. Dr. William J. Barber II (@RevDrBarber), Twitter (now X), November 8, 2017, https://x.com/RevDrBarber/status/928363113488973824.
4. Jacqui Lewis, "Fierce Love: In These Hot-Mess Times, Let Us Love Our Nation," *New York Amsterdam News*, December 12, 2024, https://amsterdamnews.com/news/2024/12/12/fierce-love-in-these-hot-mess-times-let-us-love-our-nation.
5. United States Conference of Catholic Bishops (USCCB), "A Prayer Service for Racial Healing in Our Land," 2018, https://www.usccb.org/resources/prayer-service-racial-healing-our-land.
6. Francis, *Fratelli Tutti*, encyclical letter, The Holy See, October 3, 2020, https://www.vatican.va/content/francesco/en/encyclicals/documents/papa-francesco_20201003_enciclica-fratelli-tutti.html, §116.

7. Francis, "Transcript: Pope Francis's Speech to Congress," *Washington Post*, September 24, 2015, https://www.washingtonpost.com/local/social-issues/transcript-pope-franciss-speech-to-congress/2015/09/24/6d7d7ac8-62bf-11e5-8e9e-dce8a2a2a679_story.html.
8. Francis, "Transcript."
9. United States Conference of Catholic Bishops (USCCB), "What We Have Seen and Heard: A Pastoral Letter on Evangelization from the Black Bishops of the United States," 1984, https://www.usccb.org/resources/what-we-have-seen-and-heard.pdf.
10. Subcommittee on African American Affairs, "Sr. Thea Bowman's Address to the U.S. Bishop's Conference," June 1989, https://www.usccb.org/issues-and-action/cultural-diversity/african-american/resources/upload/Transcript-Sr-Thea-Bowman-June-1989-Address.pdf.
11. Francis, *Laudato Si´*, encyclical letter, The Holy See, May 24, 2015, https://www.vatican.va/content/francesco/en/encyclicals/documents/papa-francesco_20150524_enciclica-laudato-si.html, §128.
12. "Labor and Employment: Current Advocacy Position," United States Conference of Catholic Bishops, accessed November 4, 2024, https://www.usccb.org/committees/domestic-justice-and-human-development/labor-and-employment#:~:text=CURRENT%20ADVOCACY%20POSITION,all%20those%20capable%20of%20working.
13. Francis, *Evangelii Gaudium*, apostolic exhortation, The Holy See, November 24, 2013, https://www.vatican.va/content/francesco/en/apost_exhortations/documents/papa-francesco_esortazione-ap_20131124_evangelii-gaudium.html, §204.

14. Black and Indian Mission Office et al., "Black Catholic Young Adult Recommendations from the Gathering at Xavier University of Louisiana, 11/16/2023–11/19/2023," https://www.usccb.org/resources/BCYA%20Gathering%20Final%20Report_0.pdf.
15. Barack Obama, *The Audacity of Hope: Thoughts on Reclaiming the American Dream* (Crown, 2006).
16. *Catechism of the Catholic Church*, The Holy See, accessed October 30, 2024, https://www.vatican.va/archive/ENG0015/__P8F.HTM, (§2444, 2448).
17. Francis, *Fratelli Tutti*, §66.
18. Martin Luther King Jr., "Letter from a Birmingham Jail," April 16, 1963, The University of Texas at Austin, https://minio.la.utexas.edu/webeditor-files/coretexts/pdf/1963_mlk_letter.pdf.
19. Martin Luther King Jr., "Advice for Living, November 1957," *Ebony*, November 1957, 106, https://kinginstitute.stanford.edu/king-papers/documents/advice-living-1.
20. *Directory for Catechesis*, 384, https://www.vatican.va/archive/ENG0015/__P6P.HTM.
21. Francis, *Laudato Si'*, §231.
22. Francis, *Laudato Si'*, §141.
23. *Catechism of the Catholic Church*, §1935.
24. USCCB, "What We Have Seen and Heard."

ABOUT THE AUTHOR

Ansel Augustine, DMin, is an award-winning author and Emmy-nominated producer who has worked in ministry in his hometown of New Orleans, Louisiana, and around the world for more than twenty-five years. He is a faculty member of the Institute for Black Catholic Studies at Xavier University of Louisiana, the Graduate Theological Foundation, and the Loyola University New Orleans Institute for Ministry. Dr. Augustine has served on various national boards and is a highly sought-after national speaker.

Other Books by Ansel Augustine, DMin

*Leveling the Praying Field:
Can the Church We Love, Love Us Back?*

Contributor, *African American Catholic Youth Bible*

Sunday Prayer for Teens 2014–2015

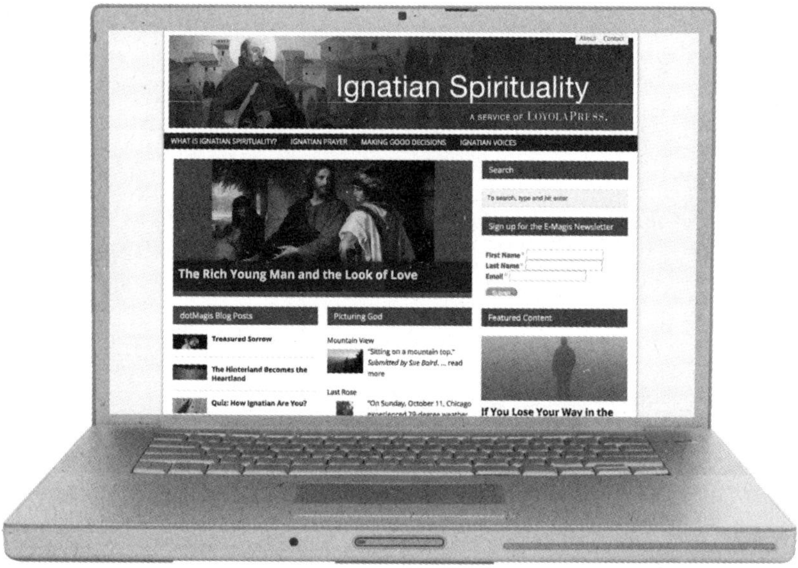

MORE BOOKS ABOUT **IGNATIAN SPIRITUALITY**

What Is Ignatian Spirituality?

Experiencing the Spiritual Exercises of St. Ignatius in Daily Life

DAVID L. FLEMING, SJ

In *What Is Ignatian Spirituality?* David L. Fleming, SJ, provides an authoritative yet highly accessible summary of the key elements of Ignatian spirituality, among which are contemplative prayer, discernment, and dynamic involvement in service and mission.

In twenty concise chapters, Fr. Fleming explains how this centuries-old method of disciplined reflection on God's work in the world can deepen our spiritual lives today and guide all the decisions we make.

English: Paperback | 978-0-8294-2718-9 | $12.99
Spanish: Paperback | 978-0-8294-3883-3 | $12.95

Ignatian Spirituality A to Z

JIM MANNEY

With *Ignatian Spirituality A to Z*, Jim Manney has developed a brief, informative, and entertaining guide to key concepts of Ignatian spirituality and essential characters and events in Jesuit history. From Pedro Arrupe to Francis Xavier, from Ad Majorem Dei Gloriam to Zeal, this book uncovers the rich language of the Jesuits. It will be an indispensable tool to anyone interested in Ignatian spirituality, to staff, faculty, and students at Jesuit institutions and schools, and to clergy and spiritual directors who advise others about prayer and spiritual matters.

Paperback | 978-0-8294-4598-5 | $14.95

TO ORDER: Call **800.621.1008**, visit **store.loyolapress.com**, or visit your local bookseller.